WITHDRAWN FROM THE MERTON PUBLIC LIBRARIES

Australia

Robin Mead

B. T. Batsford Ltd, London

To the people of Australia, who are much misunderstood and who, I suspect, like it that way.

© Robin Mead 1983
First published 1983

All rights reserved. No part of this publication may be reproduced, in any form or by any means, without permission from the publishers.

ISBN 0 7134 3829 0

Printed in Great Britain at
The Camelot Press Ltd Southampton
for the publishers
B. T. Batsford Ltd
4 Fitzhardinge Street
London W1H 0AH

Contents

List of Illustrations 6
Acknowledgments 8
1 Introduction 9
2 History and Culture 24
3 Flora and Fauna 34
4 Practical Notes 44
5 Australian Capital Territory 52
6 New South Wales 67
7 Victoria 83
8 South Australia 97
9 Tasmania 111
10 Queensland 126
11 Northern Territory 145
12 Western Australia 157
Index 169

List of Illustrations

Colour *(between pages 64–5 and 80–81)*

1. Little England Down Under: Cockington Green miniature village, Canberra.
2. Symbols of Sydney: Sydney Harbour Bridge and the Opera House.
3. Busts of Australian premiers dot the Botanic Gardens in Ballarat, Victoria.
4. Visitors pan for gold at the restored Sovereign Hill mine, Ballarat, Victoria.
5. Como Mansion, Melbourne: one of Australia's oldest stately homes.
6. Southern panorama: the Tasman Bridge, Hobart, Tasmania.
7. Australian seascape: the tesselated pavement and Eaglehawk Neck, Tasmania.
8. Ayers Rock, in central Australia, turns blood-red at sunset.

Black and White

Between pages 48 and 49

1. The new High Court of Australia, Canberra.
2. The bell tower, 'the Canberra Carillon'.
3. Aerial view of Sydney Opera House and Sydney Harbour.
4. Front view of the Opera House.
5. The Rocks, Sydney.
6. Emergency dental treatment by the Royal Flying Doctor Service on a sheep station in New South Wales.
7. Aboriginal tribesman.
8. Warrumbungles.
9. Koala bear.
10. Captain Cook's Cottage, Melbourne.
11. Sovereign Hill, Ballarat, Victoria.

List of Illustrations

Between pages 112 and 113

12 Christmas tree on the beach, Melbourne.
13 City tram in Collins Street, Melbourne.
14 The two faces of life 'down under' – a freckle-faced youngster and a sulphur-crested cockatoo pictured at Melbourne Zoo.
15 Adelaide Festival Centre, South Australia.
16 *Murray River Queen* on the Murray River, South Australia.
17 Barossa Valley, South Australia.
18 A Tasmanian devil.
19 Constitution Docks, Hobart, Tasmania.
20 Yachts competing in the Sydney-to-Hobart race tied up at Constitution Docks, Hobart.
21 Richmond Bridge, Tasmania.
22 Tessellated pavement, Eaglehawk Neck, Tasmania.
23 Port Arthur, Tasmania.
24 Beach at Heron Island, Great Barrier Reef, Queensland.

Between pages 128 and 129

25 Fossicking on Heron Island, Great Barrier Reef, Queensland.
26 Among the coral at Marineland, Green Island, Queensland.
27 Dreamland, near Brisbane.
28 Dunk Island, Queensland.
29 Rented yachts in Whitsunday Passage, Queensland.
30 Victoria Bridge, Brisbane.
31 Weird rock formations at the base of Ayers Rock, Northern Territory.
32 Aerial view of Ayers Rock.
33 The Olga Mountains, Northern Territory.
34 Aboriginal cave painting, Northern Territory.
35 City skyline from Swan River, Perth.
36 The baobab tree near Wyndham, Western Australia, whose hollow trunk was used as a prison.
37 The Pinnacles, Western Australia.

Maps

General map of Australia and Tasmania   10–11
The Great Barrier Reef   136

Acknowledgments

The author would like to thank the Australian Tourist Commission in London, Melbourne, and Sydney – and particularly the former director in London, Ian Kennedy, and his successor Ron Hewett – for their encouragement, advice and assistance during the researching and writing of this book. He is also indebted to Qantas (the national airline of Australia), to the internal airlines TAA and Ansett, and to the tour operators Thomas Cook, for providing invaluable travel and other facilities.

In addition, he would like to thank the individuals listed below, who provided background and local information, hospitality, or other assistance – and sometimes a combination of all three:

David Andersen, Bill Bostock, Pat Boyce, David Brown, Bob Bulfield, Jennifer Cochran, Ken Corbett, John Dare, Patrick Dunch, George Gibson, John Hamilton, Len Hitchen, Lionel Hogg, Kenneth Westcott Jones, John Lovesey, Bruce Lutwyche, Sir Phillip Lynch, Kate McKillop, Helen and Tom McMurray, Alan McNab, André Maestracci, Maureen Millar, Ruth Mindel, Nina Nelson, Jill and Tom Pascoe, Jim Rankin, Bernie Schulz, Bert Skinner, Ken Smith, Paula Tebbs, and Brian and Lucy Twomey.

The author and publishers would like to thank the following for kind permission to reproduce their photographs: the Australian Capital Territory, for nos. 1 and 2; the South Australian Department of Tourism, for nos. 15 and 16; the Queensland Department of Tourism, for no. 30; Sovereign Hill Goldmining Township, for no. 11; and Dreamworld Productions, for no. 27. Numbers 18 and 33 are from the author's own collection, as are all the colour plates. The remainder of the photographs were all kindly loaned by the Australian Tourist Commission (no. 36 is by Brian McArdle).

The maps are by Patrick Leeson.

1 Introduction

In the age of jet travel, Australia – that vast, still half-unexplored continent and country on the other side of the world, which used to be referred to dismissively as 'down under' – is suddenly finding a new place high up in the European consciousness. Instead of a month's voyage by boat, it is now only 26 hours' flying time away from the principal European capitals. It is sunny, rich and uncrowded – with 15 million people and $7\frac{1}{2}$ million cars. It has its summer when Europe has its winter. Lots of Europeans, especially Britons, Italians and Greeks, have emigrated to Australia and made their homes there. Air fares have fallen in relative terms, and look like continuing to fall as competition increases between the major international airlines. In short, Australia has started to come into the holiday reckoning for Europeans – many of whom have relatives living there, so that they have an 'excuse' for digging into their pockets and setting off on an adventure of a lifetime.

All the surveys in recent years of where Europeans would most like to travel have put the United States and Australia at the top of the list. The United States is already having – perhaps one might almost say 'has had' – its boom in tourism from Europe. Now the tourists are looking farther afield – to the land of kangaroos and koalas, of natural wonders like the 2000-kilometres long Great Barrier Reef and the towering Ayers Rock out in the middle of nowhere, and of beautiful cities like Sydney and Melbourne and of boomerangs and bikinis. But they see a snag.

Australia has almost deliberately created for itself an image which is distinctly unwelcoming. Its entertainers depict it as a land of beer-swilling layabouts with an undying hatred of 'bloody Pommy poofters' and other unsavoury residents of the northern hemisphere. Australian male expatriates, doing their almost obligatory world tour and settling for a while in the bed-sit land of London's Earl's

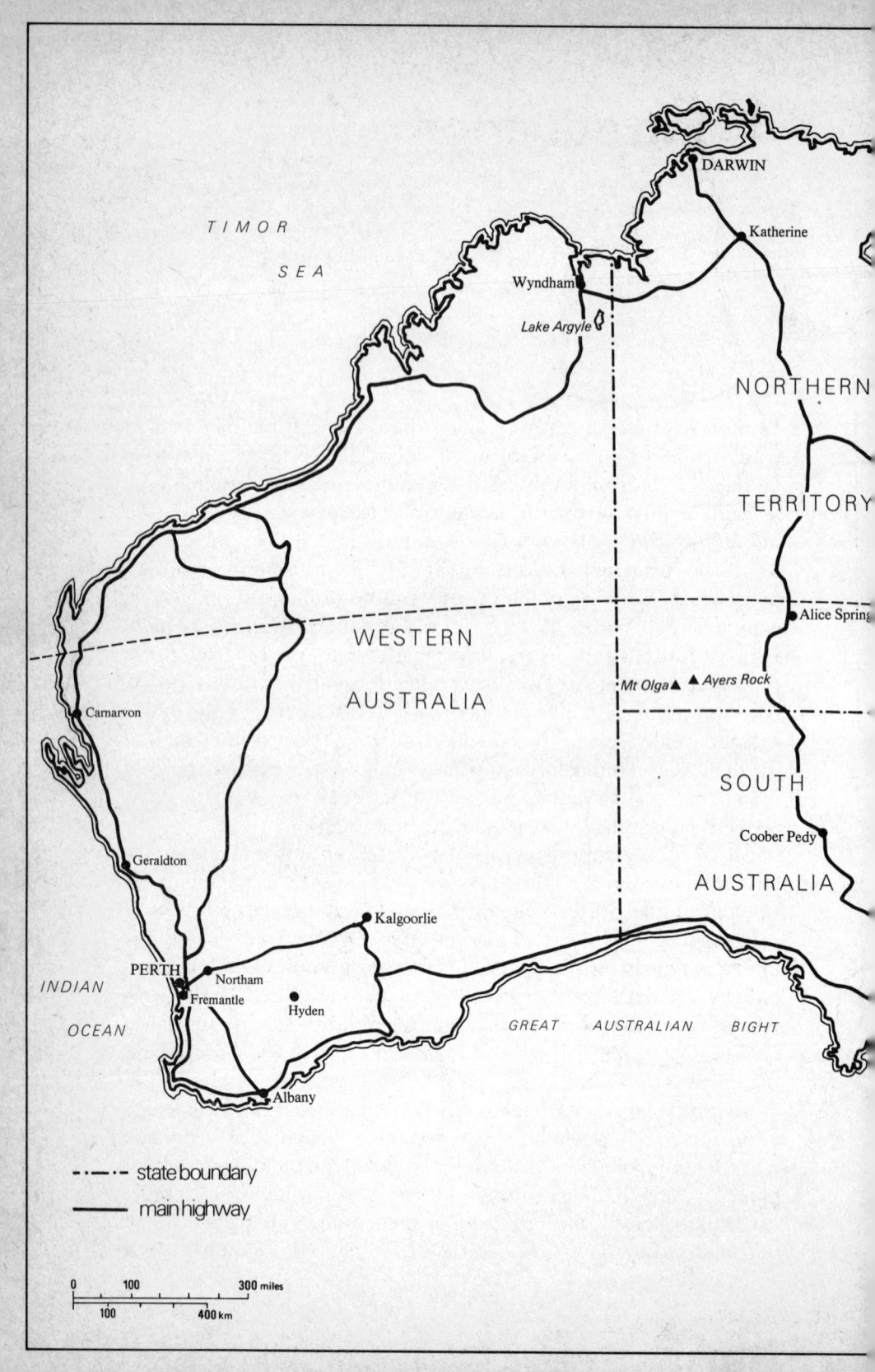

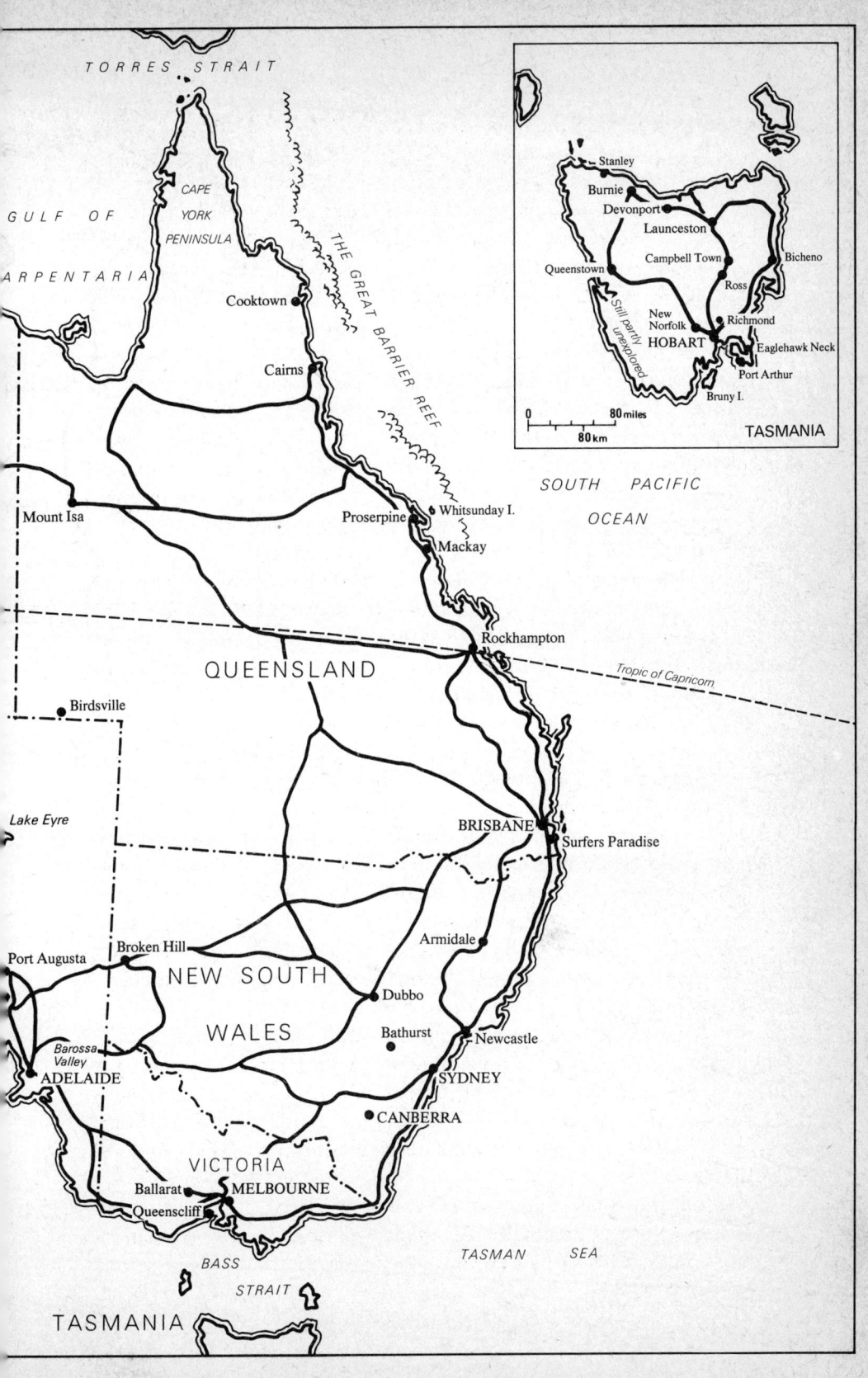

Introduction

Court, exaggerate their accents to the level of back-street Sydney, call for another 'tinny' of beer, eye the local 'sheilas' (girls, who come high on their list of priorities, but not as high as beer), profess a total disinterest in anything remotely cultural, talk endlessly about cricket, and look forward to ending the evening with a punch-up.

There is a fascinating theory that in presenting this unattractive face to the world, Australians are indulging in some serious self-protection. They know that they are extremely lucky to have a country like Australia. They enjoy all the benefits of western civilisation, yet are sufficiently far away from where that civilisation was born to have been able to avoid some of its less welcome aspects (like petty crime, organised crime, pornography, snobbery, and nuclear weapons). They are aware that the natural advantages which they and their country enjoy must attract increasing interest from the rest of the world – so they keep that world at bay by presenting as rough an exterior as they can muster.

Be that as it may, they have succeeded in convincing many would-be visitors that a trip to Australia would be a somewhat hazardous undertaking. Rough exteriors don't come much rougher than that presented by an Australian 'ocker'. A neighbour whose son had emigrated to Australia once told me that he could never go and visit that son because he was convinced that, within five minutes of landing in Australia, he would be involved in a fight. 'I couldn't stand being called a "bloody Pom",' he said. 'And I couldn't stand getting in one of those huge beer-drinking schools, where it is an insult not to stay and buy your "shout."' His wife had different fears. She firmly believed that her son had, for reasons which she found unfathomable, gone to live in a sort of arid wasteland with a couple of aboriginal stockmen as his nextdoor neighbours and nothing growing for miles around except a solitary eucalyptus tree. The fact that the youth in question was living in a seaside suburb of Adelaide did nothing to dispel these beliefs.

So what is the basic truth about Australia? What is it *really* like.

It is a big, brash, beautiful country – with people to match. It is ultra-modern, but because of its long history before the Europeans discovered it, Australia, the world's oldest continent, has a strange air of timelessness about it. And, above all, it is one of the friendliest places on this Earth.

True, the Australians will rib a British visitor about his or her origins – just as they will an Italian, American, or any other non-Australian. The British are probably their pet hate: for historical

Introduction

and constitutional reasons, because they think Britons put on airs and graces, and because they detest any hint of class (Australia claims, with some accuracy, to be a classless society). But I have never found this to be anything more than a conversational gambit; a gentle teasing which is, Cockney-style, a prelude to friendship. Give back as good as you get, do it with a smile, and the chances are that you will get a slap on the back and a 'You'll do, mate' – a high accolade.

True, Australians like a drink or two – and a lot of that drinking is indeed done in 'schools' in which to miss one's 'shout' is both an insult to one's hosts and a confirmation of their worst fears about non-Australians. But the beer comes in tiny, beaker-sized glasses (often called 'middys', although the names of various glass sizes vary from state to state) which never seem to hold sufficient to slake a tropical-sized thirst. And having a beer in Australia is even more of a social occasion than it is in England: you would have to be a dedicated drinker, or in singularly ill-chosen company, to end up legless.

Australia has been a male-oriented country ever since it was first settled, and if there is a real drawback to the country today it is that chauvinism is still prevalent. The expatriates who put beer before girls are not necessarily joking, for that really is the order of priorities in some circles and some places. Women are also made unwelcome in some pubs and bars (a few still exclude women altogether). But that attitude is changing fast, and mostly persists only in country areas.

But if the image of the chauvinist Australian has an element of truth about it, the image of the uncultured Australian could not be more inaccurate. Australians are the world's most avid theatre, concert, recital and opera-goers – as the nightly queues outside the Sydney Opera House serve to demonstrate. And in case one should be tempted to dismiss Sydney as unrepresentative, because the Opera House is a tourist attraction, I would cite the concert halls, art galleries, theatres and auditoriums which in recent years have sprung up everywhere, from the major cities down to small mining communities. These buildings are not there for reasons of local prestige: they are there because the public demanded them. And the public do not go to concerts, or to look at paintings, because it is the 'done' thing: they go because of a genuine love of music, or a genuine interest in art (a factor which has produced the patronage behind the flurry of modern Australian painting).

Introduction

Sport, of course, has an even greater following than the arts. Cricket is the national game and although a great many men (and women) play the game, it is primarily a spectator sport. The states play each other during the summer for the Sheffield Shield, and Australia plays Test matches against other cricketing nations – notably England, when the mythical Ashes (see Chapter 7) are at stake. There is no greater thrill for an Australian than to watch Australia beating England in a Test match in Sydney or Melbourne – so yes, Australians do talk about cricket. They talk about their other major spectator sports, too: Australian Rules football, horse-racing, and rugby and soccer. But most Australians also practise one or more sports of their own – sailing, swimming and tennis are probably the most popular; a lot of youngsters spend a great deal of time surfing; and golf is popular – although not as popular as in Europe or in the United States of America. A lot of emphasis is put on keeping fit generally, and in a country with an equable climate that is probably a more pleasant pastime than it might be elsewhere in the world. You will see joggers in every city park and on every beach.

Finally, one must dismiss the violent image. Australia does have its rough pubs, of course (although some of these have become tourist attractions in their own right, and now seem to be struggling to keep their tough image), and the crowds at some sporting events can become a trifle over-excited as the day wears on and the pile of empty beer cans grows. But the average Australian male is – although he will hate me for saying so – a gentleman: friendly, polite, and courteous. He is probably fairly well off, lives comfortably, and has lots of outdoor interests on which to expend both his money and his energy. He therefore has neither the time nor the inclination to go looking for trouble. So the visitor is unlikely to come across any problems, whether they be hostile natives or crime. Australia seems to be remarkably crime-free: in country areas they look at you askance if you bother to lock your front door, let alone your car, while in the cities street crimes like mugging are virtually unknown. Major cities have their 'red light districts', and indeed may even feature them as tourist attractions, but in European terms they are both safe and harmless.

If all this suggests that the Australians are a healthy, suntanned, hospitable people, who may pull your leg a little when they meet you but will none the less be glad to know you and proud to tell you about, or show you, their magnificent country, then I have done

Introduction

what I set out to do. Although Australian society is in a constant state of change, as immigrants pour in and the wealth-providing minerals and national products pour out, it does have an identity. En masse, it can remind one of pre-war London's Cockneys: the people are gregarious, noisy after a drink or two, and believe in working hard and playing hard. They have a strong sense of community spirit, a lot of grit, and a lot of determination. They are not interested in who you are, but they are interested in what you are. If you want their real friendship, then you will have to earn it, but, once given, that friendship is a bond as close as any family tie. Indeed, Australian 'mateship' – coined to describe the bond of mutual reliance formed by, say, a couple of prospectors in the outback – is a highly-prized national tradition.

'Mate' is, anyway, a common form of address in Australia – just one of the many words and phrases which Australians are in the process of making their own. Some of the more extreme examples of 'Strine' are invented as jokes, and I suppose it is possible that a few of them will actually enter, and remain in, the language. Other phrases are regional – an oddity in a country where the accent hardly varies from coast to coast. But for the most part the slang of Australia is simply a colourful, idiomatic way of speaking which abbreviates as many words as possible and gives the English language a little local colour. A recent advertisement for Foster's lager, a popular Australian beer, published only half tongue-in-cheek, read: 'G'day sport. When yer out doin' battle with the elements, riding the surf on Bondi or on a walkabout in the outback, yer gizzard gets drier than a little joey's pouch. There ain't nothing better to sink yer fangs into than a schooner of Foster's – she's a real beaut drop.' 'G'day' is a universal greeting, replacing both 'Hello' and 'How are you?' Everybody really is 'sport' or 'cobber' and 'beaut' is an expression of approval. 'Fair dinkum', the archetypal Australian expression, really does exist, and means 'true' or 'genuine'. If a word can be shortened, then it is, so 'Australia' becomes 'Oz', Alice Springs becomes just 'Alice', and Tasmania is universally known as 'Tassy' (pronounced 'Tazzy'). The temptation to be a little irreverent here is irresistible: thus St Patrick's Cathedral, in Melbourne ('Melbun') is unfailingly referred to as 'St Pat's'. 'Bloody' is widely used as an adjective, and does not attract the approbation that it would in Britain, A 'galah' or 'drongo' is a fool, you are never ill or injured but 'crook' and a job in which you don't have to work very hard (the kind of job which, according to Australians, every Briton holds down) is a 'bludge'.

Introduction

The list is endless, but the meanings are usually clear enough – and one suspects that the latter is one reason behind the continued introduction of Australianisms: the Australians would prefer it if their version of the English language raised a few more disapproving eyebrows and was a little more incomprehensible to outsiders.

Australia's outdoor image has already been mentioned, and is widely known. Most of the major cities are on the coast (seven out of every ten Australians live in the cities or their suburbs, and nine out of every ten live on the coast or within very easy reach of it) and outdoor sports – particularly water sports – are very popular. Couple this with a high standard of living (the cost of living is similar to that in Britain and Europe, but wages and salaries are usually considerably higher), and you have a country which is very pleasant to live in – a nation in which more people own their own homes than in any other country in the world, in which there is one car for every two people, and where the harbours are crammed with boats. Even the inactive take camping or caravanning holidays – either to remote stretches of coastline, or to the national parks and the parched interior.

The climate is ideal for this sort of life. Summer is, of course, in the European winter (Christmas Day in Australia is usually spent on the beach, even though roast turkey and plum pudding are still the traditional fare), and vice versa. The north of the country is tropical: hot and humid all year, and with distinctive wet and dry seasons. Brisbane is sub-tropical, with very hot summers and no frosts or snow in winter. Sydney and Perth are not strictly sub-tropical, but although the weather is more European than in Brisbane, these cities can get very hot in summer and frosts or snow are again rarities. Melbourne and Adelaide are temperate, with four distinct seasons, their fair share of rainy and sunny days, and occasional chill winters. Tasmania has a climate similar to that of northern Europe – although it can be remarkably dry (regions of Australia, like the centre, which one would expect to be drier, total up their rainfall figures fast when it does rain, because the tropical intensity of their storms means that several inches of rain can fall at a time).

The oddities of being south of the equator – the Southern Cross shining out of an unfamiliar sky, and water going down the plughole the wrong way – ensure that the European visitor to Australia will always be aware that he or she is a long way from home. But at least the surroundings should be familiar to Britons: Australians speak the same language (more or less), eat similar food, drive on the left, enjoy rapid postal and telephonic communications with the rest of

Introduction

the world (you can dial Europe direct on the telephone from most places in Australia), and have similar standards of health and hygiene to those in Britain (the water is clean and safe to drink everywhere, except – surprisingly – Adelaide).

Manners and dress are rather more casual than in Europe. Although Melbourne prides itself on a certain degree of British-style formality, in most other cities businessmen go to work in summer in short-sleeved shirts (with or without a tie), slacks or shorts, long white socks and walking shoes. In the centre and north of the country, dress styles are more casual still. Australians almost everywhere wear the clothes in which they are most comfortable, rather than what is proper, and in very hot regions they would certainly go shirtless, sockless, and possibly shoeless for all but the most formal of occasions.

Evening wear is just as casual. Australian men like their women to wear a nice dress (or 'frock'), and high-heeled sandals, but they themselves will still go jacketless and tieless. Smart restaurants, which almost anywhere else in the world might insist on a jacket and tie, instead post notices at the entrance proclaiming 'No jeans or thongs' (flip-flop sandals). Formal evening dress is hardly ever worn, not even for the opera.

For sport, or on the beach, it is very much go-as-you-please. There is a delightful trend towards topless sunbathing on major beaches all over the country – but the majority of women still prefer to protect their charms from the public gaze. Nude sunbathing and swimming are reserved for special beaches set aside for the purpose.

The Australian political and legal systems are based on Britain's, but the former is complicated by the country's federal system, under which each state has its own parliament and retains a certain degree of independence under the national – or federal – government in Canberra. State politics have rather more rough-and-tumble than politics anywhere in Europe, and these antics are gleefully reported by a highly vocal and irreverent Press which takes the view that anyone giving himself airs by going into politics is asking for all that he gets. The local newspapers make fascinating reading, and are a real power in the land.

Unlike Britain, Australia has a written constitution. This can be changed only by agreement of both Houses of Parliament, plus a majority vote by the population in a referendum in which at least four of the six states (New South Wales, Victoria, Tasmania, Queensland, Western Australia and South Australia) vote in favour.

Introduction

Like Canada, Australia retains close institutional links with Britain, and the Queen – represented in Australia by a Governor-General and six State Governors – is also Queen of Australia. In the words of the government: 'This derives historically from Australia having achieved independence through constitutional processes rather than through a unilateral declaration of independence or a rebellion.' There has been something of a move towards republicanism in recent years, and the possible appointment of a president. But loyalty to the Crown remains strong, and so does loyalty towards Britain as the mother country. Australia was undoubtedly shocked by Britain joining the European Economic Community, but has now come to terms with that and still supports Britain on most major foreign policy decisions. Australia has fought with Britain in two world wars.

The Governor-General is the head of state and the country's chief executive, with the nominal power to summon, prorogue and dissolve Parliament, assent to (or reject) Bills, appoint ministers and judges, set up Departments of State, and act as commander-in-chief of the armed forces. In practice, however, like the Queen in Britain, he acts only on the advice of ministers in virtually all matters, and the Governor-General himself is appointed by the Queen only on the advice of the Australian Government. The six State Governors perform similar roles in their respective states.

The Australian Parliament has two Chambers: the House of Representatives (or Lower House) and the Senate (or Upper House). National elections for the house of Representatives are held every three years, and the leader of the political party gaining a majority of the 124 seats becomes prime minister. As in Britain, the prime minister selects a Cabinet of ministers, and this becomes the country's senior policy-making body. The Senate, on the other hand, is modelled on its American counterpart, and its members (who represent each state in equal numbers, regardless of the size of the state's population) serve a six-year term after being elected.

Most state governments are also made up of two Houses, the Legislative Assembly or House of Assembly (Lower House) and the Legislative Council (Upper House). Queensland and the Northern Territory have only a Lower House. As in the national Parliament, the states each have a premier who is the leader of the majority in the Lower House. State assemblies control education, transport, law enforcement, health services and agriculture.

There is also a network of local government bodies, whose make-up and powers vary from state to state.

Introduction

Every citizen over the age of 18 has full voting rights in national, state and local elections.

Besides the six states, Australia consists of the Northern Territory (which does not yet have full statehood, and is partially administered by the federal authorities) and the Australian Capital Territory around Canberra. Australia also has under its wing as 'territories' the former penal colony of Norfolk Island, 1676 kilometres northeast of Sydney, which has a self-governing population of about 1800 people; the Cocos (or Keeling) Islands, in the Indian Ocean 2768 kilometres northwest of Perth, which have a population of 400; Christmas Island, population 264, also in the Indian Ocean 2623 kilometres northwest of Perth; and the 6 million square kilometres of the Australian Antarctic Territory.

Each state has as its capital one of Australia's major cities: Perth (Western Australia), Adelaide (South Australia), Melbourne (Victoria), Sydney (New South Wales), Brisbane (Queensland) and Hobart (Tasmania). All are delightful cities, and each has earned its 'capital' status by being in the forefront of European settlement in Australia. Each is fully described in the relevant chapter, under the heading of the state's name, in the pages which follow. Although the majority of present-day Australians are of European origin (the country still operates, albeit very unofficially, a highly selective immigration policy; but in recent years international events, such as the Vietnam War, have changed this and brought in a number of South-East Asian immigrants), it is important to say something at the outset about Australia's original inhabitants, the aboriginals. Australia has about 160,000 aboriginals today. Originally there were twice that number, but in the first waves of European immigration they were driven from their ancient tribal lands and hunting grounds (in Tasmania they were wiped out altogether). Now the national government has a special Department of Aboriginal Affairs, concerned with the advancement and welfare of these indigenous people, and in recent years the Aboriginal Rights Movement has become a power in the land and the demarcation of certain tribal areas has been recognised and enshrined in the nation's laws.

The aboriginals are thought to have inhabited the continent for about 40,000 years (see also Chapter 2), and in that time they had become completely attuned to their often hostile environment. But they have been less successful than the American Indians in adjusting to Western civilisation, and although some have made a

Introduction

place for themselves in society, most of them – despite intensive education schemes and special laws which make due allowance for their ancient tribal customs – prefer to remain on special reserves, the majority of them in the Northern Territory.

But they have, entirely unwittingly, had a considerable influence on the development of modern Australia. Many Australian place-names are either old aboriginal names or else derivations of aboriginal words. Their history and artefacts are of intense interest to archaeologists; their legends and art have found a place in Australian culture; their country lore has assisted in the opening up of the outback; and their cause appeals greatly to the young, the idealistic – or perhaps just the unselfish.

The aborigines are a mysterious people. They have had the practicality to live off a sparse land for thousands of years, yet they are deeply superstitious. They are skilled hunters, using the boomerang and the throwing stick (a V-shaped wedge used for giving a spear greater impetus) to great effect, yet they are basically peaceful and put up little resistance to the taking over of their land by the white man. They were and are skilled artists, who have left Australia covered with countless rock and cave paintings, yet they have always been content to be nomads and in 40,000 years did virtually nothing to lift themselves out of the Stone Age, let alone actively to improve the quality of their life. Their ancient tribal beliefs are so strong that tribal law still supersedes the laws of present-day Australia, and tribal links are so strong that an aboriginal who is expelled from his tribe will simply wander off into the wilderness to die. They have some odd powers, too, almost certainly based on psychosematics. There are many recorded cases of tribal elders 'pointing the bone' at an offending member of that tribe, which is supposed to act like a curse and ensure the recipient's early demise, and Western medical science being brought to bear to save the victim's life. The offender almost always dies, and the doctors can never establish a valid medical reason for his death.

It may be that learning to 'point the bone' would be a useful skill to acquire and bring home from a holiday in Australia. A rather easier aboriginal skill to learn, however, is throwing the boomerang – and a carved boomerang is a very good souvenir of a visit to Australia anyway.

Australia and the boomerang are as inextricably linked in the public's mind as Australia and the kangaroo. However, the boomerang did not originate in Australia. Both the ancient Egyptians and

Introduction

the North American Indians are known to have used boomerangs for hunting. What the Australian aboriginals did was invent the returning boomerang.

This was done both by carefully planning the aerodynamic shape of the boomerang, and throwing it with a flick of the wrist that gave it a farewell spin. In the hands of an expert, the boomerang would fly in a semicircle, strike the thrower's quarry or adversary, then complete the circle back into the thrower's hand. No doubt there are still aboriginals who hunt with the boomerang, but today the boomerang is a plaything and throwing it is a national Australian sport. There are annual boomerang throwing championships in several states, and at various tourist centres in Australia visitors can try learning to throw it too. It is not as easy as it looks: a boomerang thrown incorrectly may climb into the air like a runaway model aircraft, or crash on to the ground and break – and it certainly won't come back. But expert throwers can make the boomerang describe a 45-metre circle and end up back in their hand, spin in small circles, or even hover in the air. If you want a boomerang for throwing, rather than for hanging over the fireplace at home, buy carefully: most cheap souvenir boomerangs have nice carvings or paintings on them, but are aerodynamically unsound.

The aircraft which flies you to Australia (very few visitors go there by sea nowadays, although passenger ships do still serve Australian ports) will be rather more airworthy than a souvenir boomerang. Besides cutting down on flying time and the number of stops required en route from Europe or the United States, modern jet aircraft have made the trip to Australia as safe and as comfortable as possible.

Qantas, Australia's excellent (and very safety-conscious) national airline, links Sydney, Melbourne, Perth and Brisbane with London, as well as with other European capitals, major cities on the American mainland and Hawaii. Qantas's daily flights are supplemented by other principal European and American airlines, and in recent years a number of South-East Asian airlines have got in on the act too – often offering cut-price fares.

The flight from London to Sydney currently takes about 25 hours, including two stops. One can break the journey en route, in the Middle East and/or Singapore, but airlines charge you heavily for the privilege of leaving their flight for a day or two and rejoining another one later, and it is probably best to grit your teeth and get the journey over with. At least there is room to sleep on modern,

Introduction

wide-bodied aircraft, and the service on Qantas and its main competitors is excellent. International flights connect with internal flights to other centres – Adelaide, for example, although Adelaide is in the process of becoming an international gateway in its own right – and international passengers often qualify for cut-rate internal air fares.

Visitors to Australia from Britain, and most other countries, require a visa, which should be obtained before setting off. There are no airport taxes on arrival, but Australia does levy a hefty departure tax on all travellers, so do not spend all your Australian currency before getting to the airport on the final day of your trip. Australian currency is, incidentally, based on the Australian dollar, similar in value to the US dollar. The Australian dollar is divided into 100 cents, and the coinage is similar to that used in Britain (the Australian 20 cent coin, for example, looks like a British 10p piece).

Most internal travel is by air, because of the vast distances involved and the often poor roads. There are two major internal carriers, TAA and Ansett, and many smaller state or local services. Airports are uncrowded and informal, and flights unfussy as in the United States. You can check in 20 minutes before an internal flight without causing the authorities, or yourself, any distress. Officially you are restricted to one piece of hand baggage on internal flights; unofficially the rules are lax.

Although Sydney and Melbourne are the main entry airports, there is a growing enthusiasm for Perth, which is only 18 hours and one stop away from London. The internal airlines are co-operating with this idea enthusiastically, so that TAA, for example, have an onward flight across Australia to the Great Barrier Reef, via Alice Springs – which enables visitors to see Australia's greatest natural wonders without having to pass through any of the principal cities of the southeast.

There are train services connecting all the principal cities in the southeast, as well as good suburban rail services in those cities, while long-distance trains cross the continent to Perth and run north from Adelaide to Alice Springs (see also Chapter 11). Car hire is easy (overseas drivers will need to produce an international licence), petrol is cheap, and Australia drives on the left like Britain. But long-distance inter-state driving is not recommended for holidaymakers: the distances are immense, and in some areas the roads are not asphalted and are subject to flooding.

Perhaps the best way of getting around in Australia is to buy one of the 'add-on' inclusive tours, from Sydney to the Great Barrier Reef,

Introduction

for example, which can be bought in Britain before departure from firms like Thomas Cook, or which are operated by any number of companies in Australia. These are usually of a very high standard, and their all-in price represents a considerable saving on anything similar that you could organise for yourself because the bulk-buying power of the operators enables them to negotiate hefty travel and accommodation discounts.

These tours serve to highlight the variety, and contrasts, of Australia. Besides its coastal cities and famous beaches, the country has sophisticated resorts like Surfers Paradise; endless deserts; unexplored outback which can be fully seen only on safari-type camping expeditions, using four-wheel drive vehicles with extra fuel capacity; mountain ranges with winter snowfields greater than those of Switzerland (and a rapidly growing skiing industry); tropical rain-forests; ghost towns; vineyards; wide rivers (boating excursions and holidays on the Murray River are increasing in popularity); and a whole host of weird and wonderful natural phenomena.

There is no other country anything like it in the world, and Australia's long-term potential as a tourist destination must be immense if only because it offers every kind of holiday and caters for every taste – but does so at prices which, once you are there, are generally slightly lower than in Britain (clothing and consumer goods tend to be more expensive than in Europe, but tourist necessities – like accommodation and restaurant prices – are generally lower).

Would-be visitors can obtain a very informative free booklet about Australia, called *Holiday Guide*, from the Australian Tourist Commission in London (Heathcote House, Savile Row, W1 or Melbourne (324 St Kilda Road, Melbourne, Victoria), and the ATC can also help with all additional information. State tourist offices, which are represented in the major cities, can provide on-the-spot information and assistance. Britons planning an Australian holiday should contact Qantas (49 Old Bond Street, London W1), or a tour operator like Thomas Cook (Thorpe Wood, Peterborough PE3 6SB, or branches).

2 History and Culture

Australia's past stretches back so far, back into those distant times when the past really is dim, and from which painstaking work by scientists has only recently started to produce a glimmer of light, that the mind finds it hard to take in the time scales involved. For a start, Australia is the world's oldest continent: a continent which once possessed mountain ranges higher than the Himalayas. And time has reduced those mountains to an almost flat desert from which the remnants of the mountains – like the monolithic Ayers Rock and the Olgas, in the Northern Territory – still protrude.

Archaeologists and geologists are now investigating the continent thoroughly, their work having been made harder both by the sheer size of Australia and by the fact that large portions of it have been explored and opened up only in the last century. Even today, there are parts of Australia which no white man, and perhaps no human being, has ever seen. Perhaps there always will be. But it has already been shown that the continent's rocks and sedimentary strata go back to the very formation of the planet Earth, and fossils have produced the world's earliest known life forms.

One of the world's first inhabitants was an algae organism which lived in Australia 3500 million years ago. Its fossilised remains have been found deep in the earth – but, uniquely, its descendants live on today. For identical algae have been found in Hamelin Pool, Shark Bay, on the coast of West Australia.

A strange jellyfish, fossils of which have been found in the Flinders Ranges, was perhaps the first of the larger organisms which we would recognise today, to appear on the scene. And it was in Australia, 400 million years ago, that sea creatures may first have set foot on land – for in the Gippsland region of Victoria there have been found the fossilised footprints of the ichtyostega,

History and Culture

half fish and half mammal, which was the first known amphibian to have developed a backbone and roamed both the seas and dry land.

Because Australia has been an isolated continent for so long (there may once have been a land bridge across to South-East Asia), evolution followed a different pattern from the rest of the world. Australia had its dinosaurs, like everywhere else in the world. It once had a giant relation of the present-day wombat, the diprotodon, whose remains were found by Sir Thomas Mitchell, Surveyor-General for New South Wales, 100 years ago. But it was the marsupials who flourished, along with oddities like the platypus (see also Chapter 3).

Man did not appear until about 40,000 years ago – and, like today's settlers, he was an immigrant. The forefathers of the aboriginals settled in Australia because of its plentiful fauna and freshwater food, but where they came from is not known. Until quite recently it was thought that there had been two or three distinct 'waves' of immigration, 10,000 years ago and 7000 years ago – at least one of them being from the Indian sub-continent or South-East Asia, and one of a group of lighter-skinned people whose only known relatives are the Ainu aborigines of Japan. But, in 1967, the half-cremated skeleton of Lake Mungo Woman was discovered, and this is believed to be at least 34,000 years old.

Lake Mungo Woman is now known to have built clay ovens, ground flour from seed, eaten freshwater mussels and emus' eggs, and to have caught, killed and eaten kangaroos. But then her descendants were still living exactly that way as little as 100 years ago. As Professor Jack Golsen, of the Australian National University, puts it: 'Australia was the most conservative and least inventive province of the Stone Age world, making no significant contribution to the history of mankind.'

With no history, and little culture, to provide clues, the mystery of the origins of the aboriginals may never be solved. They seem to consist of three separate racial types, and some experts believe that the only people with similar characteristics to at least some of the aboriginals are the Sinhalese of Sri Lanka. But another expert at the Australian National University, former journalist Dr Alan Thorne, says the aboriginals are a totally individual race – not Caucasian, not African, and not Oriental. 'They are one of the great unmixed races of this world,' he says. 'They are themselves. They are aboriginal.'

The aboriginals themselves are not much help in identifying their origins. They can offer in evidence only the legends of the period of

History and Culture

prehistory which they call 'The Dreamtime'. These strange and wondrous stories are passed on verbally from father to son, and also feature in the aboriginal rock and cave paintings which can be found all over Australia. But they are often unintelligible and it is doubtful whether they can ever be related to hard facts.

True, some stories tell of voyages to Australia by the earliest aboriginal settlers, but they tell only of the voyagers coming from 'a land beyond the sea' or from 'the central part of the world'. Other old stories are of the aboriginals becoming marooned on Australia by rising seas (which might fit in with geological evidence, but still offers no clue as to the aboriginals' forebears), and of fighting turbanned enemies. But other tales tell how white ants released the first man from the earth, and how he killed a giant snake from whose belly came all the features of the Australian landscape: trees and rocks, rivers and plains, birds and animals. And many stories tell of mythical beings of whom the aboriginals are the direct descendants; each mythical being having created a part of the country in which his descendants now live, and to whom the aboriginals are linked by myth, lineage and environment. This belief helps one to understand the aboriginal religion in which one is totally connected with one's surroundings.

In his book, *The Dreamtime*, Charles P. Mountford writes: 'Any white man who has travelled alone with a group of aboriginal men, in places far removed from the haunts of other white intruders, will soon become aware of the links between these people and their country and the affection which they feel towards it. Everything that they see about them is reminiscent of their creation and proof of the ancient stories; the hills, the rocks, the conformation of the land, the waterholes, the trees, and even, in some places, the grass between the trees.

'Their fundamental belief is that all their secular activities, tribal ceremonies, and laws that govern both secular and ceremonial behaviour, were decreed by the mythical creators of the long-distant past.

'The aborigines live in a realm of unchanging behaviour, extending from mythical times, through the present and on to the distant future. To the aborigines, there never has been, nor will there ever be, any change in their lives. The myths that support these philosophies provide the aborigines with a reasonable explanation of the world in which they live; the stars above them, the natural forces of wind, rain and thunder and the plants and creatures that provide them with food.'

History and Culture

• More than that, the aboriginal myths are remarkably accurate when it comes to describing far-off parts of Australia. Aboriginals who have never been into the interior have accurately forecast what white explorers would find there. This is because the old stories tell of the creation of particular features of the landscape, as well as the creation of man and the other creatures of the Earth. But this apparently scientific knowledge goes hand-in-hand with an ignorance of basic biology (until the arrival of white explorers, aboriginals believed that babies were born when a spirit decided to become human, and selected a mother for itself), and superstitions such as a belief in evil spirits (the *mamandis*) and harmless ones (the *mimis*). Death is not a natural event – it is, says Charles Mountford, always due to an enemy's magic, and must therefore be avenged. The spirit of a dead person returns to its original surroundings.

Aboriginal men – who have to undergo long, often painful, and searching ritual initiation before they are accepted as tribal elders – still 'go walkabout' (i.e. abruptly leave a job or a home) because this connects them with the Dreamtime of their ancestors. For them, the Dreamtime is not necessarily a time in the past; they can still relate to it through going back to their tribal lands. This explains, at least in part, the indifference which the aboriginals have shown towards Western culture, because to them this alien culture has little or no significance.

While the aboriginals were at a physical, if not a metaphysical, halt in their development, Europeans had long believed that there might be a large, unknown land mass on the opposite side of the world. Their reasons for this belief were not particularly scientific: they thought that, without such a land mass, the Earth would unbalance and fall over. But as early as the second century AD, maps were drawn which included this unknown land. It was called 'Terra Australis Incognita' (the Unknown Southland).

In the fourteenth century Sir John Mandeville, the extraordinary explorer who was perhaps the world's first travel writer, and whose book, *The Travels of Sir John Mandeville*, is a mixture of fascinating fact about the places he did visit and fiction about the places he did not, thought that the opposite side to Britain on the flat but circular Earth contained the Garden of Eden. It was a view which the aboriginal inhabitants of that Earthly paradise might well have shared. It was not possible to reach that far land, wrote Sir John, because the way was barred by mountains, deserts and rushing rivers. 'Many great lords have assayed with great will many times for

History and Culture

to pass by those rivers towards Paradise, with full great companies. But they might not speed in their voyage. And many died for weariness of rowing against the waves. . . .'

Two centuries later, Portuguese ships exploring the East Indies may have sighted the northern coast of Australia. But in 1606 Australia was officially discovered by European explorers when Willem Jansz of the Dutch East India Company charted 322 kilometres of that northern coast. Jansz was followed by a series of Dutch, Portuguese and British navigators, all of whom charted stretches of the Northern and western coastline, and in 1642 Abel Tasman discovered the island which he named Van Dieman's Land (later to be called Tasmania). Those early explorers were unimpressed by what they saw. Far from discovering Sir John Mandeville's Garden of Eden, they reported that they had found 'the barrenest spot upon the globe'.

That view was changed dramatically by an Englishman, Captain James Cook who, on 29 April 1770, anchored in Botany Bay, close to present-day Sydney. He found a green and pleasant landscape which he promptly claimed for Britain and King George III, and which he christened New South Wales. He even found a native population who were not particularly hostile – although one did throw a spear at him. He noted in his log: 'These people may appear to some to be the most wretched on earth, but in reality they are far happier than we Europeans. They live in a tranquility which is not disturbed by inequality of condition, the earth and sea furnish them with all things necessary for life.' Aboriginal Land Rights claims notwithstanding, those wise words might be thought still true today.

A member of Cook's expedition was Sir Joseph Banks, who on his return to Britain drew the government's attention to the suitability of the new-found land for relieving the pressure on Britain's overcrowded jails. And on 26 January 1788, a fleet of 11 ships under the command of Captain Arthur Phillip landed at Sydney Cove to establish the first British colonial settlement in Australia: a settlement made up of 740 officers, 30 women, 13 children – and 759 convicts.

The Australians of today are not proud of this beginning. Perhaps it accounts for their occasional anti-British outbursts (although, when the chips are down, it would be hard to find a more loyal ally than Australia). It certainly gives rise to the riposte that their convict ancestors were, by a process of natural selection, both cunning and tough. In fact relatively few convicts would have survived the harsh

History and Culture

discipline and appalling conditions for long enough to earn their freedom, settle in Australia and raise a family. Altogether, about 100,000 convicts, men and women, were transported to Australia between 1788 and the middle of the nineteenth century, but what they did was provide the labour force for the brave and hardy families of pioneer settlers who chose to accompany them.

Phillip, who believed that New South Wales would eventually prove to be 'the most valuable acquisition Great Britain has ever made', returned to England in 1792 leaving the new colony in the hands of Major Francis Grose, the father of modern Sydney. But anarchy and lawlessness increased in the city, and in 1806 the disciplinarian Captain William Bligh, infamous leading character in the episode of the mutiny on the *Bounty*, was appointed governor and sent out to restore order. He was promptly seized by a group of officers who had been growing rich on a flourishing black market in rum. But the 'Rum Rebellion' was the last straw for officialdom in London, and Lachlan Macquarie was despatched to Sydney to take over the governorship at the head of a Scottish regiment. The penal system was promptly eased to allow well-behaved convicts a 'ticket of leave', and many stayed on to settle legally, happily, and voluntarily in their new homeland.

The penal colonies of Sydney and Tasmania were complemented by settlement along the more fertile regions of the southeastern coastline. Transport was still principally by sea, and there were few roads. Also, the interior of the country was seen as infertile and inhospitable, and there was always the fear that the aboriginals might oppose by force any settlement inland (although, in fact, this happened only in isolated instances in northern Queensland and Western Australia). Flinders sailed right round the continent in 1803, and explorers gradually made their way into the interior of the country: in 1813 William Wentworth crossed the Blue Mountains west of Sydney; between 1827 and 1829 Charles Sturt charted the Darling River; and in 1841 Edward Eyre crossed the Nullabor Plain into Western Australia. But the interior was to hang on grimly to at least some of the mystery which it retains to this day: in 1848 the Leichardt expedition, attempting to cross from Queensland to Western Australia, disappeared without trace; and in 1860 Burke and Wills were also to die attempting to cross Australia from south to north.

Perhaps Australia would have remained something of a backwater, but in 1851 gold was discovered in New South Wales, and the

History and Culture

Great Australian Gold Rush was on. Gold strikes in Victoria, near Melbourne, followed – and the country's population doubled in 10 years as fortune-hunters, entrepreneurs, and plain hangers-on flooded in from all over the world. They brought with them a certain amount of lawlessness which the police were hard put to contain, and in the 1870s bushrangers like the Kelly Gang, led by the notorious Ned Kelly, found easy pickings in the bullion convoys and new, gold-rich communities. But the railway and the telegraph had come to Australia, and together they outpaced the bushrangers' horses. The Kelly Gang, and its less famous imitators, were hunted down and brought to justice.

The population of Australia had reached one million in 1858, and although the pace of immigration slowed after the Sydney and Melbourne gold rushes, it was boosted again by the discovery of gold in Western Australia in 1882. New South Wales, which had achieved self-government in 1855, was followed by the other states, and on 1 January 1901 the states were federated into the Commonwealth of Australia (see also Chapter 5). Australia fought with the Allies in the First World War; in 1917 the trans-Australian railway linking the east and west coasts of the country was completed; and in 1918 the population reached five million.

The early 1930s were marked by an acute depression in Australia, and recovery was slow. In 1939 Australia again followed Britain promptly into the Second World War, and for much of the war it feared invasion as the Japanese swept through South-East Asia. Darwin was bombed by the Japanese in 1942 (see also Chapter 11), and Japanese miniature submarines infiltrated Sydney Harbour. But, these incursions apart, Australia escaped relatively unscathed, and in the immediate post-war years the country experienced a boom both in its economy and in the influx of immigrants.

In 1971 a national census suggested that there had been three million immigrants from 60 countries since the end of the war, over one-third of them British. But that figure also included nearly 300,000 Italians, 160,000 Greeks, 130,000 Yugoslavs, 110,000 Germans, 100,000 Dutch, 66,000 Irish, 60,000 Poles, 30,000 Americans and 13,000 Canadians.

This European influx was partly countered by 170,000 Asian immigrants – a proportion recently increased significantly by Australia's acceptance of refugees from Vietnam – and 62,000 Africans. It all adds up to a predominantly European culture, and that European culture is predominantly British. But the mix is

History and Culture

sufficiently varied to ensure that Australia today is, to British eyes at least, a pleasantly cosmopolitan country, and one which intends to stay that way.

Cosmopolitan influences are, however, not responsible for one or two curious aspects of Australia. History has given today's Australians a desire to cut the pompous down to size, and a healthy disrespect for authority. It is very noticeable that the police keep a low profile (which they can afford to do in what is, essentially, a very law-abiding country), and that – except perhaps in Canberra – bureaucracy is far from rife: both, perhaps reactions against a colonial past. This, plus the 'mortality' of officialdom, politicians and folk heroes of both the sporting and artistic variety (Australians believe that people who are put, or who put themselves on pedestals are just asking to be knocked off them), suggest a classless society – and Australia would claim that it has just that. Everybody considers themselves to be middle class. And it would seem that the country's considerable wealth is fairly evenly divided, with a very high proportion of home ownership and car ownership, and plenty of leisure. But there are pockets of poverty, not least among the aboriginals, as well as a sort of social aristocracy. And the trade unions remain very active and are led, so older Australians will claim, with some truth, by 'trouble-making' immigrants, often from Britain.

Australia's cultural heritage is principally European, and the country retains exceptionally close links with Britain as well as with the rest of Europe, the United States and the Commonwealth countries, especially Canada. But in recent years both its geographical location and the realities of commerce have forced it to pay far greater attention to its neighbours in South-East Asia and Asia generally (Japan is now Australia's principal trading partner) as well as other developing countries in the Third World. For this reason, the country is uniquely able to play a role as a mediator in Third World issues, and is held in enviable respect worldwide despite its Western ties. This role is something which one might reasonably expect to increase in future years, especially as uncommitted nations take note of the attitudes which the younger generation in Australia are taking towards issues of conscience, such as nuclear armaments. The federal system of government makes the portrayal of thinking on issues like these fit in with whatever the beholder wants to see: for a state government, for example, can take an extreme view while the national government's view remains unchanged – and Australia can appear to be sitting on the fence, and on either side of it, at one and the same time over almost any issue.

But that should not be taken to mean that Australia is not able to make up its mind on international issues. It often speaks its mind rather more effectively than other nations. And it is well able to look after itself: its National Defence Force is made up of an all-volunteer army, the well-equipped and expanding Royal Australian Navy, and the versatile Royal Australian Air Force. The close military links formed with New Zealand in two world wars remain, and Australia officially sums up its defence policy as the protection of Australia and its territories and lines of communication while remaining 'mindful also of her natural associations with the Western strategic community' and maintaining 'her concern for the security and development of South-East Asia'.

Australia's immense mineral wealth and other natural resources have been matched, since the end of the Second World War, with a marked expansion in scientific and technological development – things by which the government sets great store. There can be little doubt that, as a result of this, Australia will eventually become one of the world's leading industrial nations as well as one of the richest.

Education, including special schemes for migrant and refugee children and for aboriginals, receives similar close attention. Higher education possibilities are expanding rapidly, and Australians no longer have to study abroad if they are to reach the highest level of educational attainment. The nation's social welfare services include pensions for the aged, invalid, widowed and lone parents; sickness and unemployment benefits; maternity and family allowances; and a health insurance programme. Again, there are special welfare services for the aboriginal population, and for immigrants. Health services – a two-tier system of private treatment and community health programmes – include the nationally funded Royal Flying Doctor Service (see also Chapter 11).

Although the roots of Australia's culture are European, the environment, the country's history, aboriginal culture and the influence of Australia's neighbours have all contributed to the development of distinctively Australian trends, and the vigour and originality of the arts in Australia will come as a surprise to visitors.

In particular, a distinctively Australian school of painting has developed, and a number of Australian artists have become world-famous: among them Sidney Nolan, Russell Drysdale, Arthur Boyd, Albert Tucker, Tom Roberts, Frederick McCubbin, Fred Williams,

History and Culture

John Olsen and Brett Whiteley. The state capitals all have large public art galleries, and there are a growing number of regional art centres.

Film-making is popular, and such films as *Picnic at Hanging Rock*, *Storm Boy*, *The Chant of Jimmie Blacksmith* and *Breaker Morant* have received worldwide showing and worldwide acclaim. There is a strong literary tradition too, and Australian poets in particular have enjoyed considerable success since the end of the Second World War. Alan Moorehead, Jon Cleary, and Morris West are among authors who have won international recognition.

The country supports eight fully professional orchestras and a national opera company in addition to state opera companies. Sponsored visits to Australia by famous overseas orchestras have been enthusiastically supported. There are about 30 theatre companies nationwide, and a national ballet company.

And the crafts flourish, too – from aboriginal arts, which get national protection and support to preserve their individuality, to a long list of activities which get national grants and which include ceramics, weaving, dyeing, macramé, glasswork, leatherwork, batik, woodwork, enamelling, jewellery-making, lapidary, paper-making and embroidery.

It all adds up to an Australia which is not as the outsider tends to picture it: a country in which the best things in life rub shoulders with wild, untamed countryside. But herein lies a danger. Because one is often in a Western-style environment in Australia, one tends to forget that the harmless-looking ocean is the Pacific Ocean – full of powerful currents and man-eating sharks; or that the call of the unexplored interior has lured many travellers to a lonely death in a land where the sun is hot enough to kill and the next water-hole, let alone the next petrol station, may be hundreds of miles away.

It is a wonderful country, and one which is full of unexpected delights for the tourist. But it is also a country to be treated with respect: Phillip's laudatory comments about it may have been correct to the point of under-statement, but the earlier explorers who were repelled by what they saw as a hostile continent may have had a point too. Australia is not tamed yet – and, God willing, it never will be.

3 Flora and Fauna

Is the Tasmanian tiger, the last one of which is believed to have died in captivity in Hobart in 1933, really extinct? Or is it, as many naturalists are now beginning to believe, the world's rarest mammal, still surviving in the unexplored depths of the bushland of Tasmania?

A few years ago, former Australian wildlife ranger John Veasey was driving along a remote track in the wild, mountainous northwest of Tasmania when he saw a four-legged, dog-like creature, with 'a tail which seemed to be an extension of its body', loping along beside the road. The sighting lasted only a few seconds, but Veasey says: 'It was a creature the like of which I have not seen before, and I have seen all the wild animals indigenous to Tasmania. I am not saying it was a Tasmanian tiger – but we can hope.'

Since then Veasey has had another sighting. And he and leading Australian naturalist Harry Butler are just two of the people now planning extensive expeditions in search of the tiger. The trouble is that in the dense and impenetrable woodland of the Tasmanian wilderness, where a walker can get hopelesssly lost within minutes, searchers are likely to have to wait for snow in which to hunt for the Tasmanian tiger's tracks – and snow is a rarity on the island.

The Tasmanian tiger, or thylacine, was not a tiger at all. It looked like a dog, and its hindquarters were heavily striped like a tiger's coat. But its long, heavy tail, and the fact that it carried its young in a pouch, are evidence that it was in fact a marsupial, a distant relative of the kangaroo and the wallaby. Like one other marsupial, the ferocious little Tasmanian devil, it was peculiar to the island.

In the 1850s, both animals existed in profusion, and were hunted by settlers. Over the next 80 years the Tasmanian devil, which was thought to attack farm livestock, was almost wiped out. But a natural disaster, rather than a man-made one, attacked the Tas-

Flora and Fauna

manian tiger, whose numbers were decimated by an epidemic. Since 1933, there has been no firm evidence that any Tasmanian tigers survived.

But with the Tasmanian devil population on the island back to about a million, there is hope that the Tasmanian tiger may have made a rather more unheralded recovery in the last half-century, too. And this hope is underlined by the steady flow of reported sightings from hikers, campers, and even motorists touring the remoter parts of the island. Naturalist John Hamilton, who runs a wildlife park near Hobart, says: 'A lot of people come in here and tell me that they have seen a Tasmanian tiger. I believe them, because there is a remarkable similarity in the reports. Not too many people know what a Tasmanian tiger is supposed to look like, yet all their descriptions seem to fit.

'There is a lot of really thick bush in Tasmania, lots of places where no man has ever trodden and perhaps where he never will. I believe there are Tasmanian tigers out there, but looking for one is like looking for a needle in a haystack. Perhaps the best we can hope for is a footprint, but the Tasmanian tiger seems to have one thing in common with the real tiger: it will make a detour of many miles just to avoid a patch of mud. If it snows, however, and we can find a trail to follow, who knows what there might be at the end of it?'

Rediscovering an animal that everyone thought had been dead for 50 years really would be a conservation coup. And if 'conservation' sounds an odd word to apply to a country richer in wildlife than any other outside Africa, it is important to point out right from the start that the variety and number of indigenous plants, birds and animals in Australia is due entirely to the fact that the continent has been isolated from the rest of the world for so long. A corollary of this is the fear of what could happen to Australia's unique flora and fauna if some dreaded disease was imported into the country from elsewhere in the world. Passengers flying to Australia on board the jets of the national airline, Qantas, are already treated to a brief film lecture from naturalist Harry Butler about what steps are vital to preserve the countryside and its inhabitants, and the need not to import into the country any possibly diseased plant, vegetable, meat or animal which might cause a catastrophic epidemic. If this seems unnecessary, then it is important to emphasise that the Australians are being, if anything, under-cautious. Experience has taught them that imports of flora and fauna are defintely not always wise: rabbits, introduced into the country by white European settlers as a food

Flora and Fauna

source, flourished to such an extent that the animal is now a continent-wide pest. This has given rise to a popular myth about there being a 'rabbit fence' stretching for hundreds of miles across the centre of the country; there is no such thing, but there is, in some places, a dingo fence, built to protect livestock from the indigenous wild dog which aboriginals have occasionally tamed and keep as a domestic pet and guard, but which mostly runs wild – dingo fence notwithstanding – all over the country.

In a nation where both flora and fauna are remarkably benign – a few snakes and two species of spider (the funnel-web, distinguished by its peculiar web, and the red-backed spider, which has warning red spots on its back to clearly indicate the venom of its bite) excepted – the dingo is still feared by a few ignorant or superstitious natives and some travellers. It will certainly attack lambs and small mammals, but stories – backed up by recent well-publicised court cases – that it will take babies or young children are pooh-poohed by experts. It shuns humans and human habitation, and will not tackle any domestic dog. But there are certainly a lot of dingos in Australia, particularly in the northern half of the country, and the casual traveller may see them quite frequently in country areas, or even in the bush quite close to outlying suburbs. Like the fox in Britain, the dingo will immediately make itself scarce when spotted.

Indeed, the most fearsome animal in Australia is not the dingo, but the aforementioned Tasmanian devil. Once thought to attack livestock, the devil has now been vindicated, for it feeds only on carrion. But, uniquely in Australia, the devil (to be found only on the island of Tasmania) will turn and fight if cornered – and with teeth capable of biting through a bone eight centimetres thick, it is not too particular about what it tackles. The devil looks and sounds exactly like a small, infuriated dog. In fact, like many of Australia's best-known mammals, it is a marsupial, and carries its young in a pouch. If you leave it alone, it will leave you alone.

King of the marsupials is, of course, the kangaroo. Every non-Australian knows what a kangaroo looks like, for it features in children's picture-books the world over, is a popular resident of zoos, and even has a place – along with the emu – on Australia's national coat-of-arms. What the visitor is not quite prepared for, perhaps, is to see 'roos' running about in the wild; there are lots of them, for example, in northern Australia, and in the area around Ayers Rock. They are also to be found in wildlife parks and

Flora and Fauna

preserves all over the country – of which the best and most famous is probably Kangaroo Island, a popular excursion from Adelaide.

Kangaroos are remarkably tame, and very inquisitive, even in the wild, so they were – quite literally – easy meat for the aboriginals, who used them, and often still use them, as a source of food. There are millions of them in the wild, even to this day, ranging from the small varieties seen in herds around farms and homesteads in the southern part of the country to the big red kangaroos of central Australia. Balancing on their long, heavy tails, and leaping along on their powerfully-developed rear legs with their forepaws dangling untidily in front of them, they can move at up to 30 mph and constitute an unusual and unexpected road hazard in country areas. The warning 'Watch out for kangaroos' printed on road maps is no joke: an adult big red kangaroo, as big and heavy as a man and travelling at speed, can make a nasty dent in a car.

The kangaroo, like its usually smaller cousin the wallaby, is a grazing animal, and the herds wander wherever they can find grass. Kangaroos can be approached in perfect safety (in fact in many areas, particularly Kangaroo Island, where they are very tame they may approach you first). But don't let dogs near them, particularly if the kangaroos might have young in their pouches: the kangarooo is quite capable of sticking up for itself, and its muscular rear legs, with sharp claws at the end, have been known to disembowel dogs.

Young kangaroos – or 'joeys' – are delightful, but they are surprisingly hard to spot unless their mother is resting. They do not often leave the safety of the mother's pouch, and they leap back into it at the first sign of the unusual. The mother's mammary glands are inside the pouch, enabling the joey to feed there, and naturalists have recently discovered that the young are born only at times when conditions are best suited to their survival. The female kangaroo has a unique ability to conceive but then delay development of the foetus until, for example, it finds adequate grazing.

Because it is such a peaceful animal, the kangaroo is often selected to share a paddock in game parks with wallabies and with the huge, ungainly, flightless emu – an untidy-looking bird whose spindly legs support a hefty body, long neck, and tiny head that seems to be all beak. Emus share with kangaroos an intense

Flora and Fauna

curiosity about all that is going on around them, and in game parks the visitor intending to feed the birds may well find an emu or two coming up and helping themselves to the goodies.

The most popular Australian mammal, however, is the cuddly koala bear – the grey, furry, tailless inhabitant of the eucalyptus treetops. Despite its name, the koala is not a bear at all, but another marsupial. Although the sharp-eyed may spot them in the wild, nestling in the uppermost branches of the tallest trees, they cannot easily be approached simply because of their inaccessibility. But in wildlife parks all over the country, and particularly the Lone Pine Koala Sanctuary, near Brisbane, which is probably the best, they can be picked up by their keepers, and by visitors too.

Having your picture taken cuddling a koala is one of the prime attractions of a holiday in Australia. And the koalas really do snuggle up in your arms, exactly like an affectionate – if somewhat hefty – baby, gazing at you sleepily with big button eyes and chewing meditatively on a twig of eucalyptus leaves. The only un-babylike moment is when you try to pass the koala back to its keeper, for it will clutch nervously at your shoulder with a set of surprisingly sharp claws. If it were not for its feeding habits, and its very strictly protected status, the koala might well be the world's most popular pet; but koalas are extremely difficult to rear, or even keep, in captivity because they are extremely fussy eaters. They live exclusively on the leaves of eucalyptus trees, but will feed on only a few varieties of the tree and even then may choose to reject what looks like a perfectly acceptable meal. In captivity, they can rapidly starve themselves, or be starved, to death.

But in a land of inoffensive animals, the koala is probably the most inoffensive of all. This, and the koala's enthusiasm for spending as much time as possible either asleep or dozing, has given rise to a theory that the eucalyptus leaves ferment in the animal's stomach, and that an adult koala is therefore in a state of permanent intoxication. You may hear this theory being earnestly expounded in some wildlife parks by keepers who perhaps share the koalas' predilictions, while in others it is dismissed as being arrant nonsense. Naturalists lean towards the latter view.

Without any natural enemies apart from man, it may well be that many species of animal in Australia have hardly known fear, and that they have therefore been able to develop the friendly innocence which we normally associate only with idealistic pictures of the Garden of Eden. But if Australia is the Garden of Eden, it has

Flora and Fauna

managed to come up with some very strange inhabitants indeed. What could be stranger, for example, than a duck-billed platypus? When explorers first discovered the shy, elusive platypus, living around quiet country streams, they could not believe their eyes: it had fur like an mammal, webbed feet and a bill like a duck, swam like a fish, laid eggs like a reptile, and after the eggs had hatched it suckled its young like a mammal. Naturalists established that the platypus was indeed a mammal, and that its bill was a flattened and elongated snout. But its egg laying capability, perhaps a left-over from the very earliest days of evolution, remains unique among mammals, and the platypus is sometimes known as 'the living fossil'.

The platypus can sometimes be seen in captivity, but it is very nervous and the wildlife parks which do have a specimen rarely put it on show. They can still be seen in the wild, however, and campers and walkers in the countryside of Victoria or New South Wales in particular may find a quiet half-hour spent by a stream will be rewarded with a rare sighting.

It is far from being Australia's only oddity. This is a country in which people soon get used to sharing their living rooms with darting lizards or exotic insects – sometimes very gruesome-looking indeed, but usually harmless enough. One wonders what the early settlers made of it all. What would you make, for example, of digging up a $3\frac{1}{2}$-metre long earthworm, which promptly contracted itself into the thickness of a man's wrist and which, if you cut off its head, rapidly grew a new one? There is such a creature: it is found in Victoria and is known as the giant Gippsland earthworm, or 'barking worm'. No – it doesn't actually bark (although, if it did, one might not be too surprised): it gets its nickname from the sound it makes as it manoeuvres its massive length through the wet earth. The giant Gippsland earthworm is comparatively rare, which may be surprising as, unlike most worms, it is not sought out by hungry birds – or at least, by none except the rapacious snake-killing kookaburra, whose hysterical, manic laughter is another of the more unnerving aspects of the Australian outdoors.

The list goes on, almost endlessly. Even in the urban areas of southeastern Australia you may spot an echidna, or spiny ant-eater, looking much like the porcupine to which it is not even distantly related, digging for insects. There are silver and ring-tailed possums in many city parks, while in the bush one may find such oddities as long-nosed bandicoots, wily tiger cats, the kangaroo mouse which looks like a miniature kangaroo and isn't, or the lumbering

Flora and Fauna

nocturnal wombat – a good-natured creature occasionally kept as a pet. The wombat, incidentally, is one of Australia's oldest inhabitants: archaeologists have recently discovered the fossilised remains of giant wombats which lived there millions of years ago. As the wombat lives in a hole in the ground, his mighty predecessor must have left some massive earthworks around at the time.

Altogether, Australia has 230 species of native mammal – nearly half of them marsupials. It also has a few non-natives, ranging from the aforementioned rabbit to a very large interloper which has made its home in the country's vast deserts: the camel. Camels were introduced into the country by settlers as a means of transport in the desert areas in pre-railway days, and some are still farmed and used for this purpose. Others are used for recreational purposes: carrying organised expeditions into the outback. But there are plenty more which over the years have escaped, or been turned loose, from captivity, and which have bred happily in remote parts of the country to whose desert environment they are ideally suited. Although one knows that they are there, it still comes as something of a shock for the long-distance traveller suddenly to come upon some of these beasts in the wild. There are some wild buffalo and donkeys, too – both also imported.

The Tasmanian tiger apart, it is probable that there are now no unknown mammals in Australia. But whether naturalists have yet found and identified every reptile or insect is another question. Go out into the wastelands and deserts of central and western Australia, and keep very quiet, and you may yet see something which no non-aboriginal has ever seen before. There are, for example, some very odd-looking reptiles indeed to be spotted if you are quiet enough and quick enough. The official government *Australia Handbook* states: 'The task of identifying all of Australia's endemic species of wildlife is a continuing one. Some scientists claim there could be scores, possibly hundreds, of species and sub-species still to be formally identified and listed.'

Identified so far, in addition to the 230 mammals, are 300 species of lizard, 140 kinds of snake, two kinds of crocodile, 10 species of fresh-water tortoise, and five kinds of marine turtle.

Australia's bird life is, if anything, even more exotic. With 800 different species, they require a separate book all of their own, and ornithologists would be well advised to find and obtain just that (a number of titles are on sale in book shops in Australia). But even the most inexpert of visitors can hardly fail to notice the noisy white

Flora and Fauna

cockatoos which crowd the branches of trees in Queensland and provide what is probably the world's most raucous dawn chorus; the kookaburra, or 'laughing jackass', which is an extroverted relative of the kingfisher; the untidy emu; the fairy penguins of Phillip Island (see Chapter 7); or, if you are very lucky, the lyre-bird. The latter is something of a rarity, and is found only in the rain forests of the southeast, but it is famous for the male's mating display, when it erects its lyre-shaped tail feathers, as well as for its song and its extraordinary ability to imitate other bird calls. Other well-known bird residents of the country include bellbirds, whipbirds, and a variety of hawks, eagles and parrots as well as several members of the cockatoo family.

Australia's coastal waters and rivers contain many varieties of fish, including Queensland's primitive lung fish which can live and breathe on dry land. Anglers will find sport ranging from the game fishing which is now a growing industry in northern Queensland to superb trout fishing in Tasmania. But perhaps the seas around Australia are best explored with an aqualung rather than a rod and line, and the Great Barrier Reef, stretching down the Queensland coast and the home of hundreds of different varieties of interesting and colourful fish, is fast becoming one of Australia's top tourist attractions (see Chapter 10). It cannot be emphasised too strongly, however, that the living coral of which the reef is made is easily damaged and takes hundreds of years to replace itself, so reef 'fossicking' should not include helping yourself to lumps of coral. Quite apart from being a dangerous pastime (coral cuts hands and feet easily, and the wounds do not heal quickly), it is illegal. If you must take home lumps of coral as a souvenir of an Australian holiday, buy them from a souvenir shop.

The nation's wild flowers are spectacular, and perhaps a trifle unexpected in a country which first-time visitors find to be far more colourful than they had expected. The best-known endemic species include the waratah, the flannel flower, the desert pea, the Christmas bush, and the kangaroo paw. But, as with the fauna, the task of identifying and cataloguing the many thousands of different species of flora is a continuing one – and is likely to remain so for many years to come. Western Australia alone can already claim 6000 different species of wild flower, many of them unique. But Australians tend not to appreciate quite what a treasure-house they have in what they refer to, dismissively, as 'the bush'.

Flora and Fauna

Besides bushland, Australia has its forests, most of them limited to coastal areas where the rainfall is sufficient to sustain them. The co-existence of rain forests and sclerophyll (hard-leaved tree) forests, which are quite unrelated botanically, is an ecological curiosity – but then Australia is full of ecological curiosities. Indeed, there are some experts who believe that it may have played a major part in the early development of plant life as we know it today, and the rain forests of northern Queensland are known as 'the cradle of the flowering plants'.

In the cities and towns, you will find lots of familiar European deciduous trees – imports which seem to have settled happily enough in their new homes. But the two trees which symbolise Australia are the wattle, or acacia, which appears on the national coat of arms and is a distant relative of Europe and North America's mimosa, and the ubiquitous eucalyptus.

The eucalyptus, or gum, tree is as Australian as the kangaroo. Like the wattle, it comes in several hundred different varieties, but the eucalyptus does seem to have a remarkable aptitude for adapting itself to, and surviving in, its surroundings. Indeed, it has even adapted itself to life in many other countries all over the world, for the tough eucalyptus – once found only in Australia – has been exported to such diverse environments as the deserts of the Middle East and the southwestern states of the United States, the South African veldt, and the countryside of Japan. One can even find gum trees thriving in Britain.

About 500 different kinds of gum tree have been identified so far, and they come in all shapes and sizes. The 90-metres high mountain ash (a eucalyptus) is one of the world's tallest trees, while its stunted cousins lurk in arid regions of Australia. The jarrah (another eucalyptus) one of the world's hardest woods. Blue gum forests, such as those in Tasmania, have been (and are again becoming) a woodsman's paradise.

Most gum trees are easily identifiable because of the familiar, pungent, medicinal, aroma which is given off if the leaves are rubbbed between your fingers. They are also easily identifiable in parts of the country which have just suffered a forest fire – an ever-present danger in Australia, and one more often attributable to lightning or some other natural phenomenon than to any careless-ness on the part of man – because not only will they still be standing, but they may even be flourishing. Among its more extraordinary abilities, the gum tree – like the giant Californian redwood – has the capacity to survive fire. Indeed, fires actually seem to improve the gum tree's surroundings, by clearing away the undergrowth and other competitors for water and light. After a forest fire, the charred eucalyptus trunks will suddenly produce new leaves, and eventually new branches.

This phoenix-like skill is one which is not shared by the fast-growing evergreens with which large parts of Australia have been planted in recent years under reafforestation schemes. True, those pines may yet come in useful in a country which needs wood in proportion to its vast expanses of land; but it is equally possible that a summer storm or two could clear away the lot. Driving through Tasmania one day, one countryman eyed the featureless fir forests with distaste, and a certain amount of foreboding. 'You'll see,' he prophesied, 'This will all be eucalyptus trees one day. They are tailor-made for this environment, and pine trees are not. When they have had a fire or two, the forestry authorities may realise that Nature knows best.'

And that, somehow, sums up Australia's extraordinary wealth of plant and animal life. They may differ from anything else and anywhere else, but they all fit in with the surroundings of which they are an integral part. In Australia, nature may have taken a rather different line than she did anywhere else in the world but, as man's somewhat unrewarding attempts to intervene have already amply demonstrated, she did know what she was doing.

4 Practical Notes

Australia's cosmopolitan make-up has meant that the choice of foods is as wide as the country itself: hotel restaurants include dishes from all over the world, and in all the major cities you will find every kind of restaurant – especially so-called Australian, French, Chinese, Vietnamese, Italian and Greek.

Like everything else, Australia has undersold its culinary delights. Typical Australian dishes are seen as the ubiquitous meat pie, or the 'floater' (a pie floating unappetisingly in green pea soup), which are served as pub snacks all over the country (they may look unappetising, but I have always found them to be both fresh and delicious), or the fatty underdone steak which is looked upon as the typical outback lunch. Australian food is far, far better than that.

Because most of the cities are either on or close to the coast, the principal food is seafood – and it is the best of its kind in the world. Big, pink king prawns are almost a throwaway 'extra' on a side plate, there is lobster galore, and melt-in-the-mouth Sydney rock oysters (which you can eat safely all year round, not just when there is an 'R' in the month as in north European climes) cost a fraction of what they do anywhere else in the world. Add to that the Queensland freshwater barramundi fish (which is delicious grilled); crayfish tails; John Dory fish; Queensland mud crab; and the unfortunately named Moreton Bay bugs (which are tasty miniature crustaceans), and one can see why seafood is not only a dietary staple but is also continuingly – perhaps even increasingly – popular.

Seafood restaurants in general are quite remarkably cheap. More expensive, but still excellent value for the visitor, are the country's traditional meat dishes. The cuts are not always quite as carefully selected as they might be, but chateaubriand should appeal to European tastes, while steak and eggs, and carpetbag steak (steak stuffed with oysters) are popular. Mutton, and lamb chops, are the

Practical Notes

other principal meat dishes – again they are fattier than in Europe, but very good value. Appetisers are described on Australian menus as 'entrées', and main courses are generally served automatically with potatoes and two other vegetables. Australian diners like their meat rare, but it is a mistake to ask for it to be 'well done' as you will get it very dry – which may account for the national enthusiasm for smothering almost every dish with lashings of tomato sauce or ketchup.

Side salads tend to be unimaginative (basically lettuce, cucumber and some tired-looking slices of tomato), and relatively pricey. There is a growing enthusiasm for fast foods, but again these can be expensive compared with the more traditional dishes. The fruit, particularly pineapples, melons, paw-paws, passion fruit and grapefruit, is cheap and superb.

But let's start at the beginning. The Australian hotel or motel breakfast is a large, American-style affair, with orange juice, fresh fruit (usually tropical), crispy bacon served with tasty little sausages and runny poached eggs, toast, and tea or coffee. Australians have a fondness for smothering their toast with marmalade, honey, jam or Vegemite – a proprietary yeast extract spread similar to Marmite. Tea is as popular as it is in Britain, and similarly served. The coffee is stronger than its American counterpart.

You can lunch off a beer and a pie in the pub. The beer-drinking capabilities of the average Australian, it must hastily be added, are a self-generating myth: certainly the average Australian likes a glass, or a can (popularly known as 'a tube' of beer, but then in a warm climate, probably, so will you. But what expatriate Australians never admit is that the nation's beer – mostly pale, lager-type – is not served in pint glasses, or even half-pints. It is served in a small glass known, depending upon where you are, as a 'middy' (usually 10 ounces), a 'schooner' or a 'pony'. Ask for anything larger, and you will rapidly earn a reputation as a boozer! Most beers are locally brewed (there are more than two dozen breweries in Australia), although imported brands are available at a price, and it is always served chilled. It looks weak, but it isn't – so take care.

Australian wine is first-class. The principal wine-growing areas are in New South Wales and South Australia, and their produce compares favourably with the best that France can produce, let alone Italy, California or South Africa. Some of the white wines, and the local champagne, might taste a trifle sour to a European

45

Practical Notes

palate, but the rich, fruity clarets and cabernets are really excellent and very cheap.

When the time comes to go out to dinner, usually you have to think about what you want to drink beforehand. The majority of restaurants are unlicensed, and advertise themselves as 'BYOG' restaurants. 'BYOG' stands for 'Bring Your Own Grog' – which means just that. You take in your wine or beer (purchased from one of the handily situated off-licences, which keep restaurant hours) with you and, for a small charge, the restaurant will uncork it for you and supply you with glasses. Other restaurants will send out for drinks for their clients, again for a small corkage charge.

Every city has its seafood restaurants, 'Australian' restaurants, 'English' restaurants, and American-style hamburger restaurants. Every city also has a selection of French restaurants, which are usually good without quite coming up to Parisian standards, and Chinese restaurants which may be good and may not (try to pick a well-established one). Apart from this, the range of ethnic restaurants reflects the make-up of the local population. Adelaide and its surroundings, for example, have some truly great German restaurants, which no doubt draw a fair proportion of their customers from the local German communities in and around the wine-growing areas. Adelaide and Sydney have several first-class, and very popular, Greek restaurants. Melbourne and Sydney have a variety of Italian restaurants – some of them good, others rather mediocre. And the influx of Vietnamese refugees has led to a flurry of Vietnamese restaurant openings in Sydney – but although these are still well frequented because of their curiosity value, I have yet to find a good one.

But you may not have to eat out. Australians are warm and generous hosts, for whom the evening meal is something of a ritual. Even quite casual acquaintances will be invited to 'pop round for a drink', and such guests invariably find that the 'drink' includes a lavish buffet meal or a barbecue in the garden (or on the beach).

If you are invited to a barbecue, or any kind of meal, in an Australian home at the weekend, accept. Australians take their weekends even more seriously than the evening meal, and cities practically close down over the weekend. Even more than in Britain, the Australian's home is his castle – his escape from the outside world. He wants to be with his family, but he is more than happy that visitors should share that family occasion. In the summer he will probably head for the beach; at other times there are sporting events

Practical Notes

to watch or take part in (club cricket, tennis, racing, fishing, golf), and there are well over 250,000 yacht and power boat owners in the country. Australians remain active sportsmen (and sportswomen) far longer than they do in Britain, so don't be surprised if your 50-year-old host says that he is off to play cricket for the day or challenges you to what will be a highly competitive game of tennis.

The sports facilities are extensive almost everywhere – even Alice Springs boasts a golf course, and up-to-date squash and tennis courts. Major spectator sports are cricket (international Test matches are held in the state capitals between December and February); Australian Rules football (played principally in the southeastern states); Rugby League football (New South Wales and Queensland); soccer (played everywhere, and growing in popularity); and horse racing (Melbourne and Sydney). Betting on horse races is almost a national epidemic, and there are betting shops everywhere.

Bowls is much more popular than it is anywhere in Europe – and I am referring, of course, to lawn bowls and not to American ten-pin bowling. Even the smallest country town has its bowling greens, and there are tens of thousands of players. The sport's 'capital' is Queensland's Gold Coast.

Golf courses proliferate, too, and again there are several to choose from in and around all the major cities, ranging from public courses where anyone can play to private (and often quite exclusive) courses where you can only play as the guest of a club member. Some Australian golf clubs have reciprocal playing arrangements with British clubs.

But there are surprisingly few golf links in Australia – the Australians have better things to do with their beaches. I have yet to meet an Australian who could not swim; surfing is popular, especially on the Pacific beaches (but underwater currents can be treacherous, and there is danger from sharks, so choose a netted beach with lifeguards on duty). Skin and scuba diving inevitably have a huge following in a country with 2000 kilometres of Great Barrier Reef to explore; and yachting, which ranges from club racing in sheltered bays like Sydney Harbour to long-distance races for ocean-going yachts, is almost a religion. If they don't go sailing, your Australian hosts may still take to a boat – this time for deep-sea angling and game fishing, which is particularly good in northern Queensland waters. The mountains of New South Wales, Victoria and Tasmania also have a plethora of lakes and streams which

Practical Notes

attract anglers, as well as hikers and campers, and there is skiing in New South Wales and Victoria in winter (when the demand for facilities unfortunately tends to outstrip supply).

Hiking and camping are particularly enjoyable in many parts of the Australian countryside, and the number of devotees of these particular activities increases every year. Many Australian families own either a static caravan, usually on a seaside site, or else a towable vehicle or motor-caravan which they use for camping expeditions into the very attractive and unspoilt countryside within easy reach of cities like Sydney, Melbourne and Adelaide. Many of the mountain ranges teem with wildlife, and to camp out there under the Southern Cross is an unforgettable experience, as unique in its way as an expedition into the outback. The latter, it should again be emphasised, is something only to be taken in a fully equipped four-wheel drive vehicle.

At the opposite end of the entertainment spectrum, there is gambling. As can be seen from the popularity of betting shops, Australians love a 'flutter' – and Hobart, capital of the island of Tasmania, owes its place on the tourist map very largely to the fact that it is the site of Australia's first casino. The Wrest Point Casino, which doubles as a luxury hotel and offers nightly cabaret performances of a very high standard, always seems to be crowded with gamblers with money to burn, and a very large percentage of them are Australians rather than overseas visitors. In some states, like New South Wales and Victoria, anti-gambling legislation is strict, so perhaps the Tasmanian gamblers are indulging at least in part in the time-honoured Australian custom of cocking a snoot at authority. But it is more than that: talk to a punter in the casino – or in a small-town betting shop, come to that – and he will tell you that he likes the glamour and the thrill of gambling, that he worked hard for his money, that he intends to spend it as he wishes, and that if you don't like it then you know what you can do. He has said much the same to the government. And at least some state governments have taken note: besides a second Tasmanian casino being built in Launceston, others are planned for Alice Springs and Darwin, in the Northern Territory, and for a couple of places in Queensland, probably Surfers Paradise and Townsville.

Shopping is another holiday pastime, and in the main cities of Australia it is remarkably good. If, when you arrive in Australia, you discover that you have left something at home, there is no need to worry: almost anything that can be bought in Britain can be

1 Modern architecture on the world's oldest continent: the new High Court of Australia building in Canberra.

2 Canberra's bell tower, the Canberra Carillon, was a present from Britain.

3 Sydney sunset: the Opera House and Sydney Harbour Bridge.

4 Aerial view of modern Sydney and the famous Opera House.

5 Sydney's oldest quarter, the Rocks, has undergone renovation.

6 Emergency dental treatment at a New South Wales sheep station from the Royal Flying Doctor Service.

9 Koala bears really are cuddly – if you can catch them.

10 Old amongst the new: Captain Cook's Cottage, in Melbourne.

11 An old mining town comes back to life: Sovereign Hill, Ballarat, Victoria.

Practical Notes

purchased in Australia. But suggesting any particular bargains or souvenirs is something of a problem: most items in the shops cost as much as, if not more than, their European equivalents. Opals, and some other jewellery, are cheaper than in Europe, and aboriginal handicrafts make good souvenirs which one certainly could not obtain elsewhere. Add a cuddly toy koala or two, and the almost-obligatory boomerang, and that is about it. But beachwear is cheap; and the determined may find one or two examples of Australian humour – like a foul-smelling 'Bullshit' spray which the frequenters of some resort pubs like to produce and spray in the air when they consider that one of their fellow imbibers is talking too much, indulging in self-glorification, or telling too long a story. That might amuse the chaps in the office back home. On the other hand it might not.

In the cities, most shops and stores are open from 9 a.m. until 5 p.m. daily, and from 9 a.m. until noon on Saturdays when they then close for the weekend. In country areas shopping hours are theoretically more elastic, but in practice they may be even shorter because the proprietor may like to close for lunch and an afternoon siesta.

Many guidebooks to Australia suggest that tipping is not a common practice. Certainly this was once the case, when a tip was thought to be patronising, and it may still be true in country areas where, for example, a taxi driver who turns out in response to your telephone call may consider himself to be helping you rather than providing you with a service (not that this will deter him from charging you the usual fare). But things are changing fast, and in the main towns and resort areas tipping is certainly the custom now. You should add about 15 per cent to restaurant bills, tip taxi drivers 10 to 15 per cent of the fare (and be prepared for a mouthful of shouted abuse if you don't), and tip people like porters, too, unless there is a set charge for handling baggage as at some airports.

Your choice of clothing for a trip to Australia should, as mentioned in Chapter 1, be made with comfort in mind rather than what is 'the done thing' – because there is no done thing in Australia anyway. No particular care is necessary when packing for a trip to Australia, because of the ready availability there of anything you might need, from colour film to specialist drugs. But unexpected items which I have found essential, and which I would now take on any trip, include durable walking shoes (for wear almost anywhere except the cities and the seaside); a sunhat (never mind if normally

49

Practical Notes

you never wear a hat – the combination of hot sun and clear air can be lethal); old tennis shoes (for walking on the razor-sharp surface of the Great Barrier Reef); insect repellant (for flies and mosquitoes); and an electrical plug convertor (Australia's electrical current is 240 volts, so one can use electrical appliances safely, but their three-pin electrical sockets take a peculiar, triangular-shaped plug for which you will need a 'universal' adapter such as the Traveller, which is available in shops in Britain).

Personal effects can be imported temporarily into Australia, along with 200 cigarettes or their equivalent and a litre of spirits. There are some restrictions on audio equipment, but otherwise the holidaymaker should not be troubled by Customs regulations at the port of entry. Generally there are no health restrictions, although arrivals from countries where there are epidemics of smallpox, cholera or yellow fever will be required to have a valid International Certificate of Vaccination. The interior of arriving aircraft is sprayed as a protection against animal and plant pests and diseases, and there are strict controls on the import of animal and vegetable matter – and sometimes on their carriage between the various states. Visitors are advised to carry health insurance because, as in America, although medical treatment in Australia is readily available and of a very high standard, it can be very costly for travellers from overseas.

Visitors from Europe should also be prepared to suffer from what is, so far as I know, an incurable health hazard if they fly to Australia: jetlag. Besides the rigours of a flight lasting 26 hours or more, the body has to adjust to a very considerable time change (Australia is divided into three time zones, and the time there is from eight to 10 hours ahead of the time in Britain). A restful few days is the best antidote to jetlag, but because there is a tendency for some time to feel sleepy during the day and wide awake at night it might be worthwhile to take sleeping tablets for a short time.

In recent years, Australia has converted to a metric system of weights and measures. All distances are measured in kilometres.

Visitors to Australia travelling on a tourist visa cannot take paid employment, or engage in full-time studies, while they are there, and the visa cannot be exchanged. If you go to Australia and like it so much that you want to emigrate there, you will have to return home and negotiate with the Australian High Commission.

Information for tourists is readily available from the Australian Tourist Commission's offices in London and elsewhere (see Chapter

Practical Notes

1), but more specialist information is available from three other distinct kinds of source.

(a) *State tourist bureaux or travel centres*. The headquarters of these organisations are as follows. *Australian Capital Territory:* ACT Government Tourist Bureau, Corner London Circuit and West Row, Canberra City, ACT 2601. *New South Wales:* NSW Government Travel Centre, 16 Spring Street, Sydney, NSW 2000. *Northern Territory:* NT Government Tourist Bureau, 9 Parsons Street, Alice Springs, NT 5750. *Queensland:* Queensland Government Tourist Bureau, Corner Adelaide and Edward Streets, Brisbane, Queensland 4000. *South Australia:* SA Government Tourist Bureau, 18 King William Street, Adelaide, SA 5001. *Tasmania:* Tasmanian Government Tourist Bureau, 80 Elizabeth Street, Hobart, Tasmania 7000. *Victoria:* Victorian Government Travel Centre, 272 Collins Street, Melbourne, Victoria 3000. *Western Australia:* WA Government Travel Centre, 772 Hay Street, Perth, WA 6000. The advice that these offices can provide includes information on facilities for handicapped people.

(b) *Convention bureaux offices*. These are situated as follows. *Sydney:* Sydney Visitors' Bureau, 291 George Street, Sydney, NSW 2000. *Gold Coast:* Gold Coast Visitors' Bureau, Suite 42/43 Centre Arcade, Gold Coast Highway, Surfers Paradise, Queensland 4217. *Brisbane:* Brisbane Visitors' and Convention Bureau, 82 Ann Street, Brisbane, Queensland 4000. *Adelaide:* Adelaide Convention Bureau Ltd, 7 Pirie Street, Adelaide, SA 5000. *Melbourne:* Melbourne Tourism Authority, Nauru House, 80 Collins Street, Melbourne, Victoria 3000. *Hobart:* Tasmanian Convention and Visitors' Bureau, 142 Macquarie Street, Hobart, Tasmania 7000. *Perth:* Perth Convention and Visitors' Bureau, State Insurance House, 815 Hay Street, Perth, WA 6000.

(c) *National parks*. *New South Wales:* National Parks and Wildlife Service, 189–193 Kent Street, Sydney, NSW 2000. *Victoria:* National Parks Service, 240 Victoria Parade, East Melbourne, Victoria 3002. *Queensland:* National Parks and Wildlife Service, 138 Albert Street, Brisbane, Queensland 4000. *South Australia:* National Parks and Wildlife Service, 129 Greenhill Road, Unley, SA 5061. *Western Australia:* National Parks Authority, Hackett Drive, Crawley, WA 6009. *Tasmania:* National Parks and Wildlife Service, 16 Magnet Court, Sandy Bay, Tasmania 7005. *Northern Territory:* Territory Parks and Wildlife Commission, PO Box 1046, Alice Springs, NT 5750.

5 Australian Capital Territory

Any visit to Australia starts, naturally enough, in Sydney, Melbourne, or perhaps Adelaide, Perth or Brisbane – since they are the entry points for flights originating overseas. Canberra, the nation's capital, does not feature highly on the first-time visitor's itinerary, yet Canberra and the 911 square miles (2368 square kilometres) of land surrounding it and known as the Australian Capital Territory, are important because more than anywhere else in this vast country they symbolise the scale, the potential, the modernity and the unity of Australia. Perhaps every visitor to Australia should start his or her tour in Canberra, or at least visit the city during their stay: excepting, perhaps, Brasilia there is nowhere else like it on earth.

It is there because the conflicting claims of Sydney and Melbourne to be the nation's capital could not be resolved, and New South Wales – the state in which Sydney is situated – had even gone so far as to refuse to join the federation of states which was to become Australia unless the capital city was within its boundaries. So at federation, in 1901, it was written into the constitution that there should be a new capital, purpose-built within the state of New South Wales, and after a seven-year search for a suitable site a spot was finally chosen on the western slopes of the Great Dividing Range. It was in spectacular, green countryside, ringed by mountains and nearly 2000 feet (600 metres) above sea level; 140 miles (220 kilometres) southwest of Sydney and 280 miles (440 kilometres) northeast of Melbourne.

Today, nearly four generations later, Canberra – the only city in the world to rule a continent – still looks like a vast building site; and on the drive into town from the airport the enormity of the project can be grasped by making the brief detour up to the top of Mount Ainslie, and the Mount Ainslie Lookout. At one's feet are the glittering waters of Lake Burley Griffin, the man-made lake which is

Australian Capital Territory

now the main feature of Canberra, while around and across the lake all roads seem to be part of a triangle whose apex is Capital Hill, soon to be the home of the dramatic new Parliament House which is due for completion in 1988.

But this is no ordinary city. It has been built – perhaps 'is being built' would be a better phrase – so that hills, and trees, and greenery are features of, rather than intrusions into, the builders' work. Walter Burley Griffin, the American landscape architect who won the international competition (and a prize of about $A3500) for designing the city in 1912 and upon whose plans the layout is based, but who did not live to see those plans reach anything like fruition, would be proud of his creation.

The people who live and work in Canberra – nearly 250,000 of them, instead of the 25,000 for whom Burley Griffin originally planned – say they would live nowhere else. Certainly the city, and the satellite towns built to accommodate the huge influx of residents, have an attractive appearance and an ambience all their own. The already considerable afforestation is being steadily increased all the time with a massive tree-planting scheme; the roads are wide and often apparently semi-deserted; the comfortable homes with the sweep of green lawns in front of them are urban life personified and dumbly assert the affluent good life that Canberra can offer.

Unlike most major Australian cities, Canberra has clearly identifiable seasons. In spring, the orderly flower beds and flowering trees give Canberra a picture-book appearance; in summer the lakes and trees have a cooling effect rare in the parched hinterland of Australia; in autumn the trees put on yet another dramatic display of colour; while in winter the climate is reasonably gentle, with only a breath of the cold winds and frost which one might expect at this altitude.

Yet one cannot forget that Canberra is a man-made city: far more so than any other of Australia's cities, which have grown up and flourished around a natural port or some other form of communication or agricultural necessity. Canberra is a city built by bureaucrats for bureaucrats. It is attractive, tidy, spacious, efficient – and soulless.

Forget about a luxury hotel – there isn't one (although one or two major hotel groups are active in the city, to the extent that existing buildings are already being torn down to make way for new developments which will shortly include first-class hotel facilities).

Australian Capital Territory

Forget about a swinging nightlife; this is a town of diplomatic cocktail parties, back-garden barbecues, and early nights. You will need a self-drive hired car, or lots of energy and very stout shoes, if you are to get around to see anything, unless you have the good sense to go to Canberra on an organised sight-seeing excursion – for although there is a very great deal to see both in Canberra itself and in the surrounding countryside, distances are considerable and public transport infuriatingly scarce.

From Mount Ainslie there is a magnificent panorama across the bulky – and in the context of Canberra, surprisingly ugly – War Memorial, to the red surface of the wide, tree-lined Anzac Parade leading down to the lake and, right opposite on the far side of the lake, to the low but rather grand white-fronted edifice of the present (or Old) Parliament House. The lake has bridges across it to the left and right, neatly aligned to form the sides of the triangle which has Capital Hill as its apex. Just inside the bridges are the two major features of the lake, and to my mind two of the most attractive and dramatic features in the whole of Canberra: the futuristic Carillon, or bell tower, which stands on Aspen Island beside Kings Avenue Bridge, and the gushing 500 feet (137 metres) high water spout of the Captain Cook Memorial Water Jet beside Commonwealth Avenue Bridge.

All are worthy of closer inspection. The water jet – which is very similar in appearance to the one in Lac Leman, just offshore from Geneva – is only half of the Captain Cook Memorial, which is completed by a metal globe, three metres in diameter, standing on the lake's shoreline. The globe depicts the voyages of Captain Cook, and consists of an openwork metal ball with the land masses picked out in beaten copper. The jet itself is worked by two powerful electric motors which force water up into the air at a speed of 260 kilometres an hour, and its other principal vital statistic is that at any one time six tonnes of water are actually hanging in the air – which, apart from being a dramatic sight, makes the jet a useful point upon which to get one's bearings in a city where, despite the formal layout of the main streets, it is deceptively easy to get temporarily lost. The jet works from 10 a.m. to noon, and 2 p.m. to 4 p.m. daily, and cuts off automatically in high winds.

The Carillon, a gift from Britain to mark Canberra's fiftieth anniversary in 1963, is one of the largest in the world, and contains 53 cup-shaped bells ranging in weight from six tonnes to less than seven kilograms and arranged in four-and-a-half chromatic octaves.

Australian Capital Territory

Its Westminster chimes peal every 15 minutes and, reflected across the waters of the lake, these chimes quickly become a sound which one associates especially with Canberra. There are weekly recitals, on Sunday mornings and Wednesday lunch-times.

Lake Burley Griffin, with its 35 kilometres (22 miles) of shoreline, much of it made up of parks and nature reserves, provides some unexpectedly good city centre walking, sailing, or even trout fishing. It was formed by damming the Molonglo River and, although such a lake was an essential feature of Burley Griffin's original plan for the city, it was not actually completed until 1965: political rows, financial problems and two world wars having delayed construction work on this and many other aspects of a city which is only now beginning to feel like an entity in its own right. It is hard now to imagine what Canberra must have been like without its lake, and it is a tribute to the planners that, when flooding did finally take place, the only real amenity to disappear beneath the waters was part of the Royal Canberra golf course.

From the lakeside, every visitor should take the walk up Anzac Parade to the Australian War Memorial, nestling at the foot of Mount Ainslie. Anzac Parade, its red surface made up of crushed building bricks, commemorates the co-operation of Australian and New Zealand armed forces in two world wars, and it is the site of Australia's Remembrance Day parade every November as well as being the venue for other ceremonial occasions. Suitably enough, the wide avenue is lined with flowering shrubs from New Zealand and, behind them, Australian blue gum trees.

At the top of the parade the Australian War Memorial really is an extraordinary building, but its appeal is such that it is, after Sydney Opera House, the most popular tourist attraction in Australia. The memorial itself is a Byzantine-style, cross-shaped structure of cream-coloured sandstone brick, its Hall of Memory containing Raymond Ewers' huge bronze statue of a soldier, and three stained glass windows and a massive mosaic designed and built by a First World War casualty, Napier Waller, whose work is all the more remarkable when one considers that he undertook it despite having lost an arm. The Hall of Memory is fronted by the shallow, rectangular-shaped Pool of Remembrance, and the pool is flanked by twin colonnaded galleries containing, on bronze plaques, the names of 102,000 Australians who have died in the two world wars and other twentieth-century conflicts such as the Korean War and the confrontation between Malaysia and Indonesia.

Australian Capital Territory

But if this, the 'ground floor' of the War Memorial, is a symbol of the wastefulness of war, then the vast basements beneath it which serve as Australia's War Museum somehow seem to glorify mortal conflict. They contain room upon room of well-presented and graphically haunting relics, paintings, photographs, sculptures and three-dimensional models of Australian participation in the First World War, the Second World War, the Korean War, the Malaysian emergency, and the Vietnam War. The accent is macho rather than melancholy, and one cannot but wonder at the effect that the display has upon, say, the parties of schoolchildren who are taken there and who, assuming that they see the Roll of Honour first and the sound-and-light models of successful Australian actions second, may quickly forget the cost, in human lives, of the battle scenes they are witnessing.

One must hope that, one day, the dioramas glorifying war will be scrapped and greater attention paid to things like the 250,000 war photographs, the miles of cine film, and the thousands of books, periodicals and war diaries held in the War Memorial's library – a collection of vast historical importance. Indeed, it is probable that the full extent of the treasures which the War Memorial houses has not yet been properly grasped. Comparatively recent, for example, is the realisation that it has the world's largest collection of Victoria Crosses, and the citations which go with the medals; and that, with 8000 war paintings, sketches and sculptures by Australian artists, it contains more examples of original Australian art than any other museum or art gallery in the country.

Outside the War Memorial is a collection of heavy armaments and other relatively modern military equipment, of which the most interesting is the reconstruction of a Japanese midget submarine – made up from the remains of two which were destroyed in Sydney Harbour in 1942. The submarine serves as a dramatic reminder that Australia was very much in the front line during the war in the Pacific: it was bombed by the Japanese, and one can only hazard a guess at what might have happened if Japanese troops had ever reached the mainland of Australia. In providing such sombre food for thought, the Australian War Memorial at least serves one very positive purpose. And, fittingly, the complex closes every night to the sounding of the Last Post.

If the War Memorial unwittingly contains Australia's most extensive art collection, then by the time this book is published it will at least be rivalled by another of Canberra's important buildings, the

Australian Capital Territory

Australian National Gallery. At the time of writing, the $A25½ million building was still under construction, but director James Mollison had managed to complete a ten-year, $A50 million shopping spree by collecting for the city – and the nation – more than 2000 works of art from Australia and overseas. This collection, whose works range from Tiepolo and Cezanne to Warhol, is intended for display in the National Gallery's 7000 square metres of exhibition space, and the building itself is one of the most attractive in the city.

One of its closest rivals, perhaps, is its nextdoor neighbour, the High Court of Australia. The highest court in the land (although, constitutionally, appeals against its decisions can sometimes be made to the Privy Council, in London), it does not look at all like the sort of building in which one might expect important legal issues to be decided: it is approached by a gently sloping path alongside which a man-made stream – architects prefer to describe it as a fountain – scurries over concrete blocks which force it into swirling rivulets (it is attractive, I suppose, but it does look extraordinarily out of place); and the building's lobby is a tourist attraction in its own right, a soaring public hall reaching to a height of 24 metres with an open ramp system leading to the courts on the higher levels. The courtrooms themselves are bright and functional, and furnished in light wood. You almost expect to see counsel wearing Bermuda shorts, instead of wigs and gowns.

Another spectacular lobby is to be found in the National Library of Australia, which was opened in 1968 and therefore qualifies as one of the city's older major buildings. Surrounded by marble-faced columns, which give it an almost classical appearance, and with a Henry Moore bronze, 'Two-Piece Reclining Figure', outside it on the lakeshore, the library is a place for art lovers as well as book lovers and students, since the foyer and mezannine galleries – besides containing a constantly changing exhibition of items of outstanding interest from the library's collection – features three spectacular five-metres high tapestries by the French artist Mathieu Matégot, depicting aspects of Australian life; a massive Tom Bass copper relief above the entrance; and 16 colourful 'stained glass' windows. The windows are actually made of chunky Belgian and French glass mounted in concrete, and were designed by the Australian artist Leonard French to depict the planets.

The contents of the National Library are impressive, and already increasing at such a rate that an extension is to be added to the

Australian Capital Territory

existing building. They read like an entry in *The Guinness Book of Records*: 1,500,000 books; 92,000 reels of microfilm of books; 500,000 aerial photographs of Australia; 303,500 other photographs; 255,900 maps; 97,000 titles of newspapers and magazines; 31,000 paintings, drawings and prints; 43,000 films and video cassettes; 55,000 music scores; 360,000 sound recordings; 64 kilometres of shelving; 600 full-time staff. . . .

The figures are out of date as one types them, but they do serve to indicate the size and scope of this undertaking. And of the collection in the National Library, one must pick out such outstanding items as Cook's hand-written journal of his voyage on the *Endeavour* in 1768–71, during which he charted the east coast of Australia; a log of the voyage; several of Cook's letters; the diaries of the Burke and Wills expedition; and the papers of Australia's first prime minister, Sir Edmund Barton.

The present Parliament House is one of Canberra's oldest landmarks, for it was opened by the Duke of York (later King George VI) in 1927. It was always intended as a temporary home for the national parliament, and at the time of writing, its fate when the new Parliament House on Capital Hill is opened is still undecided. One must hope that some use is found for it, for it is an attractive as well as historic building (and the latter are, after all, all too rare in Australia), and the 25-minute tours of the building are worth taking (ask in the spacious, colonnaded King's Hall, immediately inside the main doors). Parliament normally sits on Tuesdays, Wednesdays and Thursdays, and consists of two houses: the Senate and the House of Representatives. King's Hall contains a real treasure in the carefully protected form of one of the three existing copies of the *Inspexius Magna Carta* – the document which was issued by England's King Edward I in 1297 and which finally confirmed what the original *Magna Carta*, signed by King John at Runnymede in 1215, had been intended to do: extend the protection of the law to all free men. Australian law, which is of course based on British law, still contains parts of this document.

Parliament House will inevitably be overshadowed by the magnificent new Parliament House, whose opening in 1988 is planned to coincide with Australia's bicentennial. This is a truly magnificent building, planned to melt into its hilltop surroundings yet obtrusively topped by the unique, four-legged metal flagpole which could yet become as symbolic of Australia as the Southern Cross, the kangaroo or the emu.

Australian Capital Territory

From the ceremonial forecourt, a high colonnaded vestibule curves opposite the main entrance doors, and a sculpted frieze above the entry depicts Australia's history. Immediately inside, a lofty foyer leads to the reception hall – which is to be the scene of state receptions and banquets – and to the second-level public areas. The three-level Members' Hall corresponds to King's Hall in the provisional Parliament House, and links the Senate Chamber and the House of Representatives' chamber, each of which are surrounded by offices and other facilities.

A pyramid-shaped skylight beneath the flagpole gives the Members' Hall natural daylight, while large glazed galleries along the curved walls also provide daylight for the central areas of the building. Each floor looks out on to landscaped gardens in a natural setting, and future Members of the Australian Parliament will feel as though they quite literally have Canberra, if not quite the world, at their feet.

As a contrast to such ultra-modernity, one should visit one of the oldest public buildings in the city centre: Blundell's Farmhouse, near the Carillon. This is a cottage built by settler George Campbell of Duntroon in 1858 for his ploughman, and it has been preserved and now houses a museum of nineteenth-century life in this part of Australia. The cottage is open every afternoon.

There are a number of other nineteenth-century buildings in and around Canberra – enough of them, indeed, to form an entire village were they gathered in one spot instead of being scattered around the Australian Capital Territory. They include a number of fine homesteads, a gaol, a dairy and a schoolhouse, and collectively they bear witness to the fact that Canberra's rich farming country was discovered and settled by Europeans as early as the 1820s. Many of these old buildings have been, or are being, restored under the aegis of the ACT Historic Sites and Buildings Committee and the National Trust.

The finest homestead in the territory is Robert Campbell's Duntroon, built in 1833. Campbell (1769–1846), a Scottish shipowner, was the first settler to be granted land on the site of what is now Canberra. When one of his vessels was lost while under charter to the government of New South Wales, Campbell received the land in compensation, and rapidly set about becoming something of a gentleman farmer in the style of a Scottish laird. He named his homestead after Duntroon Castle, a Campbell stronghold in his native land, and – besides Blundell's Farmhouse – another famous

Australian Capital Territory

building in the Australian capital owes its existence to Campbell, because he founded Canberra's oldest church, the Anglican church of St John the Baptist, whose traditional English lines still peep shyly through the thick trees and hedges on the corner of Constitution Avenue and Anzac Parade. Duntroon itself was acquired for Australia's Royal Military College in 1911, and now serves as the officers' mess and living quarters for the single men.

For visiting motorists, and those prepared to undertake a little touring on their own account in a hired car, the ACT Government Tourist Bureau (London Circuit, Canberra City, ACT 2601. Tel: 49 7555) issues a handy free booklet describing a range of suggested 'Drive-yourself Tours' in and around Canberra, which comes complete with opening times and potted histories. And, besides the principal buildings already described, an initial tour would take in the Canberra Planning Exhibition on the lakeside at Regatta Point, and what is perhaps Canberra's oddest – and in some ways most interesting – collection of buildings, the foreign embassies which are concentrated in Red Hill, Forrest and Yarralumla.

The Australians had considerable problems in persuading foreign countries to move their diplomatic missions to Canberra. By 1955 most of them were still situated in Melbourne, and foreign ambassadors and Commonwealth high commissioners alike were reluctant to leave that pleasant city for the new – and to many of them virtually unknown – national capital. But in that year the tough Australian prime minister Sir Robert Menzies abruptly ordered all his government departments to move to Canberra, and ensured that the diplomatic missions followed them by threatening to withdraw recognition from any diplomatic representatives who did not leave Melbourne for Canberra.

Menzies' instruction ensured the future of Canberra as the nation's capital, and also gave the diplomatic missions a unique opportunity to go in for a bit of national self-expression when planning and building their embassies. The results are now a tourist attraction in their own right, with the Italian, Japanese, South African, Malaysian, American and Indonesian embassies in particular all being built in the traditional style associated with the country in question.

The other principal city tour is the 45-kilometre drive around Lake Burley Griffin, although an alternative is to take a lake cruise (vessels depart from the ferry terminal beside the northern end of Commonwealth Avenue Bridge). The drive takes in the campus of

Australian Capital Territory

the Australian National University, lying on the lakeshore between the Civic Centre and the lookout point known as Black Mountain. This picturesque campus is open to the public, while on the edge of it are two more buildings which bear witness to the city's rapidly growing reputation as a centre of learning, science and research: the moated Australian Academy of Science, and the Australian Institute of Anatomy.

The university operates the largest astronomical complex in the southern hemisphere, with headquarters on pine-clad Mount Stromlo, only 16 kilometres from the city centre. There, a number of silver domes house a variety of astronomical equipment, and a visitors' gallery adjoining the largest telescope (a 1·9-metre giant) contains a display describing the activities of both the Mount Stromlo observatory and its sister observatory on Siding Spring Mountain, near Coonabarabran, in New South Wales.

Both observatories are handily situated close to another of the ACT's modern wonders, the Canberra Deep Space Communications Complex at Tidbinbilla, 24 kilometres farther out of town. Tidbinbilla is a major link in the United States' National Aeronautics and Space Administration's (NASA's) worldwide communications network, and has played a major role in many successful and spectacular space missions such as the lunar landings and the current long-range expeditions to the planets.

The circuit of the lake also takes in another Canberra spectacle: the Royal Australian Mint, in Denison Street, Deakin. One of the largest and most modern mints in the world (it can produce coins at the rate of 100,000 a day), this building is reponsible for the production of all the coinage of Australia – and, indeed, that of a number of other countries, too. From a long gallery lined with plate glass (to ensure that there is no pilferage), visitors may watch every stage of the minting process in what is actually Canberra's only factory of any size. An exhibition in the foyer traces the history of coinage, and the development of coin design. Presentation sets of newly minted, uncirculated coins, which can be bought in the foyer, make a nice souvenir of Australia.

On Black Mountain Lookout – one of four such vantage points around Canberra, and providing panoramic views – another stop can be made at the 195 metres high Telecommunications Tower. Designed with the visitor very much in mind, the tower has three public viewing galleries, a rotating restaurant, and a small theatre. It provides magnificent views of both Canberra itself and the

Australian Capital Territory

surrounding city, by day or night, and the region's remarkably clear atmosphere (an excellent reason for its choice as an astronomical centre) mean that this view is usually perfect. But the Telecommunications Tower has, as its name suggests, a more pressing reason for its existence than providing pleasure to the public: it is a receiving and transmitting station for radio and TV broadcasts, and telephone calls.

The latter are certainly in need of some modern technological assistance, for at the time of writing one of the major drawbacks of Canberra is that, unlike most principal Australian cities, it lacks subscriber trunk dialling links to the rest of the country, let alone overseas destinations. Add that to the poor choice of hotels, and one can see that there is plenty still to be done in making Canberra into a truly modern metropolis, let alone a capital city.

Although, as I have said, more hotel developments are planned, the city's main hotels at present are Noah's Lakeside International Hotel, the City Travelodge, the Canberra Rex Hotel, and the Travelodge Manuka. Of these, the Canberra Rex is recommended – although it is only fair to add that it lacks one or two basic facilities, such as a coffee shop serving soft drinks and snacks (you have to order them at the bar), and shoe-cleaning equipment. Still, it tries hard.

The city is better served when it comes to restaurants. The rotating Tower Restaurant, in the Telecommunications Tower on Black Mountain, is popular; as are the Red Door, in the city centre; Zorba's Lake View Tavern, in Belconnen Mall; Albert's Restaurant at the Old Canberra Inn; Willard's Steak House and Oyster Bar, in London Circuit; and the excellent Lobby Restaurant, opposite the old Parliament House. Personal favourites would be Peaches Restaurant and Bar, in Blamey Place, Campbell – an inner suburb five minutes' taxi ride from the city centre – which concentrates on what it calls 'simply good food'; and the relatively unknown Le Rustique, in Garema Place, a small, modestly priced restaurant with very good French cooking.

But I must admit that one of the nicest meals I have enjoyed in the Canberra region was also one of the simplest: a pub lunch in the George Harcourt Inn in Guneahlin, near the satellite town of Belconnen, about 12 kilometres northwest of Canberra's city centre. Owned and run by an Englishman, Michael Allen, the George Harcourt Inn is right next door to the miniature village of Cockington Green, in Gold Creek Road. As its name, not to mention

Australian Capital Territory

its menu, might suggest, the George Harcourt Inn is a modern but traditionally styled English pub – complete with a stuffed fox on the mantelshelf and toby jugs and teapots hanging from the rafters. The only concession to the pub's Australian setting is a brass plaque on the wall which warns: 'No bloody swearing'. It serves a satisfying but cheap snack lunch of bread, cheese and pickle, but to wash it down the nearest you will get to an English-style drink is draught Guinness – served chilled.

The pub shares a car park with Cockington Green, which is already well on the way to becoming Canberra's leading out-of-town tourist attraction. Designed, built, owned and run by an Australian entrepreneur with an English wife, Cockington Green is a beautifully kept miniature village containing scale replicas of English period homes and other historical buildings in a garden setting. It has the inevitable miniature railway running around it, and such is the energy of the owners that it is growing rapidly, so any description of it would already be out of date by the time you read this book. The village is open to visitors daily.

Belconnen is one of Canberra's three new satellite towns, built to house its swelling population. Like Canberra itself, it is built around a lake, Lake Ginninderra, which was created in 1976 and is one-seventh of the size of Lake Burley Griffin. The town is inevitably suburban in style and atmosphere, although it does boast what is said to be the southern hemisphere's largest shopping mall (there is a rival claimant to the title near Melbourne; although with only New Zealand, South Africa and parts of South America as competitors, the title is hardly worth claiming anyway) and one or two interesting buildings such as the ultra-modern National Sports Centre, nearby. Ginninderra, the area in which Belconnen is situated, is one of the oldest parts of Canberra, and an excursion to the area should include stops at All Saints Church in Cowper Street, Ainslie (just north of central Canberra), and the Ginninderra Falls in Parkwood, to the west of Belconnen. The church is interesting in that it was once the mortuary station at Rookwood Cemetery, Sydney, and when it fell into disrepair it was sold for £100, dismantled brick by brick and rebuilt in Cowper Street in 1958. It contains Canberra's only recorded ghost. The falls, a 10-minute drive from Belconnen, include a walk along a scenic nature trail leading to the spectacular Ginninderra Gorge and Falls.

The nature trail is a reminder that, even in such urban surroundings as these, the accent is on the outdoors. There is excellent golf in

Australian Capital Territory

and around Canberra; licence-free fishing on Lake Burley Griffin; and a number of very good nature reserves – including Canberra Wildlife Gardens, southwest of central Canberra and very close to the city, which contains native and exotic birds and animals in a landscaped environment (open daily); and the government-run Tidbinbilla Wildlife Gardens, within the Australian Capital Territory 20 kilometres southwest (also open daily).

A tour to Tidbinbilla could include a visit to Lanyon Station, near Tharwa, which was once the leading sheep and cattle-grazing property in the Canberra area. It flourished in the mid-nineteenth century, when it grew to almost village proportions and was held up as a model property. But its 12,000 acres of rolling grassland beside the Murrumbidgee River were perhaps too close to Canberra – for today it is part of the development area for one of Canberra's satellite 'new towns': Tuggeranong. The elegant homestead, which consists of 25 rooms and dates from 1859, has National Trust protection ard is being preserved as part of a recreation area – as are the gardens and outbuildings. Some of the outbuildings actually predate the house, having been built by convict labour in 1835. There is an art gallery nearby, and this is devoted to the work of Australian artists. The entire Lanyon complex is open daily, except Mondays.

The southern part of the ACT consists entirely of a nature reserve, the Gudgenby Nature Reserve, which makes up one-fifth of the area of the territory and contains an extensive part of the wild highlands of southeastern Australia. The variety of the countryside in this reserve – ranging from grassy valleys to bare, rocky mountain summits; and from swampy creeks to eucalyptus forests – mean that it contains a huge range of animal, plant and bird life, and it is an ideal spot for the naturalist, or walker. Some of the walking, however, is remarkably hard going, and visitors are warned to go properly equipped: every year enthusiastic hikers who set out into the bush wearing only sandals, shorts and a shirt end up as another statistic in the rescue services' log-books – and rescue work in this terrain comes expensive.

Weather extremes are also intense: it can be unbelievably hot on the exposed hills in summer, and in winter snowstorms can block the tracks. For these are the foothills of the Australian Alps: perhaps Australia's least-expected bit of topography. The Alps, lying only 100 kilometres south of Canberra and easily reached from the city, are a vast tract of mountains which actually have more snow on them in winter than is to be found in the whole of Switzerland.

1 Little England Down Under: Cockington Green miniature village, Canberra.

2 Symbols of Sydney: Sydney Harbour Bridge and the Opera House.

3 Busts of Australian premiers dot the Botanic Gardens in Ballarat, Victoria.

4 Visitors pan for gold at the restored Sovereign Hill mine, Ballarat, Victoria.

Australian Capital Territory

Visitors to Canberra are close enough to see something of the Alpine scenery whatever the season. The top attractions are the Snowy Mountains and the gigantic engineering achievement of the world-famous hydro-electric scheme, and the skiing centre of Thredbo. Organised coach excursions are run to the area from Canberra, while motorists can reach it via Cooma. In winter, motorists should call at the Cooma Visitors Centre to check on road conditions in the mountains.

In the opposite direction, motorists going north from Canberra can visit the area around Goulburn, at the heart of the area known as the Southern Tablelands. In Goulburn, which is only 90 kilometres from Canberra, the steam museum, Pelican sheep station and Hume Dairy are all worth seeing, while the beautiful Bungonia Gorge and the sapphire and gold mining centre of Grabben Gullen are within easy reach. The drive is a pretty one, too: it passes through rich, dairy-farming countryside dotted with historic homes, Australia's richest wool county country, and old, unspoilt Gundaroo.

And, finally, there are Canberra's beaches. With most of Australia's major cities being situated on the coast, one might expect that immigrants to the ACT might quickly start yearning for the seaside. In fact, the city's residents reply to such suggestions by pointing out that they are only a couple of hour's drive from the coast.

The coast in question is the south coast of New South Wales. And Bateman's Bay, prettily situated at the mouth of the Clyde river, 150 kilometres southeast of Canberra, has become in all but name the national capital's seaside resort. It has good beaches, and if the visitor finds them a little too crowded with Canberra folk on high days and holidays then there are plenty more little coastal towns, and plenty more beaches too, strung along the Princess Highway to the south of Bateman's Bay – places like Nowra, Ulladulla, Moruya, Narooma and Bermagui.

These ancient aboriginal place names are a reminder that Canberra itself owes its name to an aboriginal word: 'Canberry', or 'the meeting place'. It was the name given to the first sheep station on the site of what is now the capital city of Australia, and its retention was a happy idea: certainly happier than the alternative suggestions of Shakespeare, Utopia, Mathilda, Marsupiala and Myola. The latter, suggested by the American King O'Malley, who started work on building the city in 1915, was a bit of a mystery until someone discovered that Myola was almost an anagram of O'Malley.

Australian Capital Territory

What have Burley Griffin, O'Malley, and those who have come after them created? Every visitor to Canberra seems to react differently. I find it pleasantly spacious, and the lack of such eyesores as hoardings or posters (even garages and petrol pumps are hidden away down side streets) is a relief after most cities. Some of the new buildings are somewhat gaunt, and the lack of obviously ancient structures – let alone the irritating scarcity of tourist facilities – is disorientating.

But Canberra grows on you. Some of the developments being undertaken there are quite magnificent, and architecturally the city will undoubtedly be a place to be remarked upon for many years to come. As a tourist centre it obviously has an excellent future, for the time is coming – indeed, it probably has already arrived – when no visit to Australia is complete without seeing Canberra and its national treasures. One can only hope that the hotel accommodation will increase proportionately in quality and quantity.

Whether one would care to live there is another question. Unless and until one was 'accepted' by the neighbours, it could be a very lonely spot, I imagine: a bit like setting up home in a park full of priceless statuary, the full significance of which was known only to a few experts. The people who do live there are friendly enough on the surface, but slightly aloof, self-protective, hiding behind the façade of their modern houses, swimming pools, and well-defined but exclusive social life.

One of them attempted to explain this. 'I've lived all over Australia', he said, 'and there's nowhere like Canberra. I think I've found the ideal place to live. And, that being the case, why should I tell other people about it?'

Well, he could be right. There are many worse places than Canberra. But I couldn't help feeling that, in his heart of hearts, he knew that there are many better places, too.

6 New South Wales

Canberra may be the capital of Australia, and Melbourne may have illusions of grandeur which are not entirely misplaced, but there is no doubt about which is Australia's principal city: it is Sydney. Sydney is where Australia began (see Chapter 2); it is, with a population of three million (one in five of the population of Australia), the country's largest city; it is the industrial and commercial focal point of the South Pacific; and it is a major port and communications centre. It is also something more than that: it is far and away the most beautiful city in Australia, and if a world beauty contest were to be held it would be a close contender for that title too.

Nobody could fail to like Sydney, the glittering and cosmopolitan showpiece of Australia. In may ways it epitomises the country: it is modern, busy, lively, and rich. Unlike most of the other major state capitals it has not been built on the grid system – that idea was scrapped in the earliest days of its development. But no one could say that its latter-day planners have not made the most of their surroundings. With the huge, and very attractive, natural harbour as its centrepiece, it has in the familiar shape of the famous Sydney Harbour Bridge what must be one of the engineering marvels of the world – despite the fact that it is now over 50 years old. And the controversial wing-roofed Opera House, which Sir John Betjeman has unkindly likened to a group of nuns in a rugger scrum, must be one of the world's architectural wonders.

If Sydney has a businesslike air about it, it is also a surprisingly warm and hospitable place. It has its old-fashioned, trendy quarters, like the Rocks, and even its own little Soho in and around the Kings Cross district. And, of course, its beaches are superb even if Bondi Beach and Manly do tend to get a little crowded at weekends (in Australia, one notices, it is the lifeguards – not the policemen – who get younger with the passing years).

New South Wales

If time is short, take the Sydney Explorer bus (fare: about £2.50 per day), which follows a circular route and allows passengers to get on and off whenever they like and as often as they like: it is a great way to see the city. And don't miss the Captain Cook harbour cruise, which is as spectacular a half-day excursion as one is likely to find anywhere. Between them, these two tours will show you all that is best about the city, and enable the tourist who is just passing through to see the city in a day. But if possible one should plan to linger in Sydney, for time there is time well spent. It is a fascinating place.

Although Captain Cook's landfall in 1770 was in New South Wales, it was not in Sydney Harbour. He dropped anchor in Botany Bay, close to the site of the present-day international airport. It was left to Captain Arthur Phillip, at the head of a shipment of British convicts, to sail between the Heads of Sydney Harbour in 1788 and, on 26 January, to establish the first British settlement in what is now the heart of Sydney. Some of the settlement's original buildings can still be seen in the historic Rocks area.

A few years later his successor as governor, Major Francis Grose, scrapped plans for the roads of the embryonic city to be laid out on the grid system, and ruled that roads could be built anywhere as long as they were wide enough for two bullock carts to be able to pass one another. The result is that, in the older parts of the city at least, the roads twist and turn as they do in few other Australian cities, following the contours of the land and the serpentine meanderings of the harbour shore.

In 1814 a gifted convict architect called Francis Greenway was given permission, as part of a rehabilitation programme, to begin changing the ramshackle convict settlement into a proper town, and there emerged the colonial versions of English late-Georgian architecture which today form the core of the older part of the city. Examples of this include St James's Church, in Queen's Square; Hyde Park Barracks, which is now a law courts and is also in Queen's Square; Parliament House, in Macquarie Street; the Old Mint (now state government offices), in Macquarie Street; and Victoria Barracks, Paddington, where visitors can still watch the Changing of the Guard at 11 a.m. every Tuesday. The Obelisk, in Macquarie Street, is the point from which all distances were once measured.

In Victorian times, the city began to grow rapidly – spurred by the people, and the wealth, which flowed in as a result of the gold rush in

New South Wales

1851. Many of the original Victorian buildings still remain, even if they are overshadowed by the skyscraper developments of the second half of the twentieth century. They include Richmond Villa, in Kent Street; the GPO Building in Martin Place; the Custom House at Circular Quay; Sydney Town Hall, in George Street; and the Queen Victoria Building, also in George Street. A number of churches in the city – including both St Andrew's Cathedral in George Street and St Mary's Cathedral in College Street – and the Great Hall of Sydney University are good examples of Gothic revival architecture; and Fort Denison, in Sydney Harbour, is the former Pinchgut Prison which today serves as a signal and tide-measuring station.

The harbour, which is described – with every justification – as the world's most beautiful deep water harbour – is immense. It has a shoreline of 240 kilometres, and an area of 54 square kilometres. This shoreline has produced some of the world's most dramatic and sought-after private housing sites, and on a harbour cruise you will have some of Sydney's most expensive homes pointed out to you. One could pay £1 million or more for a house overlooking Sydney Harbour in one of the more exclusive suburbs – and still not have the best home in Sydney. The harbour is a very busy one, filled with commercial maritime vessels ranging from huge passenger liners to massive container ships, and with the passenger ferries criss-crossing the water all round the clock (many suburban residents find it more convenient, not to mention more pleasant, to travel to and from work by ferry, rather than trying to drive on the tortuous, and often jammed, roads). But there is still room to spare for yacht races, and it has been estimated that the harbour is home to more than 10,000 privately owned yachts and power-boats.

Sydney Harbour Bridge, the world's largest single-span bridge for nearly half a century, was opened in 1932, and its bow-shaped structure (it is known locally as 'The Coathanger') still dominates the city of which it was for so long the accepted symbol. It crosses the harbour from Dawes Point, close to the Rocks and the ferry terminal at Circular Quay (which, just to make things difficult, is not circular at all, but square-shaped), to the unattractive suburbs of north Sydney. But it is worth crossing the 503-metre long bridge, if only for the view that one gets of it, and of the Opera House behind it, from Pelican Point.

Today the Opera House, standing on Bennelong Point, on the opposite side of Circular Quay to the bridge, has replaced Sydney

New South Wales

Harbour Bridge as the symbol of Sydney, and perhaps as the symbol of Australia. Fourteen years (and innumerable quarrels and problems) in the building, it was designed by the Danish architect Joern Utzon and is one of the most original and striking buildings in the world. It cost $A102 million, it finally opened in 1973, and experts have said that compared with it, constructing the Empire State Building in New York was as simple as building a garage. Some people dislike the soaring, white, shell-shaped roofs which cover the five separate main performing halls within the Opera House complex, but most find it extraordinarily beautiful – and its light, sparkling apperance certainly offsets to perfection the dull, grey, chunky appearance of the bridge looming behind it.

More important, perhaps, it has revolutionised the cultural life of Australia. Attracted both by its prestige and by its superb facilities and near-perfect acoustics, leading artists from all over the world perform there.

The five main halls are the Concert Hall (seating 2700 people), the Opera Theatre (seating 1550), the Drama Theatre (seating 550), the Cinema (seating 420), and the Recording Hall (seating 300). There are also two rehearsal halls, many smaller rehearsal rooms, a versatile reception room, an exhibition hall, two restaurants, a souvenir shop, and a number of galleries and balconies – all linked spectacularly together by concrete and glass.

There are conducted tours of the Opera House during the day, and taking one of these tours is almost like making a behind-the-scenes tour of an airport, for the Opera House is like a small self-contained town which never sleeps, and where there is always something going on. Far better, however, to book tickets or even go and join the queue for last-minute seats and see one of the performances. As they stage symphony concerts, recitals, jazz sessions, opera, ballet, drama, chamber music, choral works, musicals, one-man shows, films and lectures there, you will have plenty to choose from. And a night at the opera at the Sydney Opera House is a never-to-be-forgotten experience – as much for one's fellows in the audience as for the performance itself. For the young people of Sydney have become followers of the classics to a degree which puts the Promenaders in Britain to shame: casually dressed (there are no white tie and tails for the opera in Sydney), they will queue for hours to watch a performance, and are obviously both extremely knowledgeable and extremely critical.

Because there is so much to see and do in Sydney, one must be selective. Sydney is so large (larger than either Greater London or

New South Wales

New York), and its attractions so varied, that one could write a book just about this city and still only have scratched the surface. But after the harbour cruise (which departs several times a day from Circular Quay), the Sydney Harbour Bridge, the Opera House, and the Sydney Explorer bus (or a walking tour), the top tourist attractions are (or should be) the following.

The Rocks are named after the rocky slopes of the west side of Sydney Cove. This birthplace of the Australian nation was the site of the first settlement but, because it was unsuitable for the construction either of proper roads or proper drainage, it rapidly became a slum: its unsanitary hovels were taverns and brothels frequented by mariners, and thugs and press gangs lurked in the dark alleyways ready to rob sailors of their money, their freedom, or both. In 1900, when plague broke out in Sydney, the Rocks area was suspected of harbouring the disease and large parts of it were burnt down. More buildings were demolished in 1924, when work began on building Sydney Harbour Bridge, and in 1957 there was further demolition to make way for the Cahill Expressway. But in 1970 the state government formed the Sydney Cove Redevelopment Authority to restore and reconstruct this historic area, and although this is a continuing process, much work has already been completed. There is a visitors' centre in the Old Coroner's Court, dispensing free maps and brochures; the State Archives, housing early colonial records; The Rocks Square, where the sandstone memorial 'First Impressions' commemorates the founders of the infant colony; Campbell's Storehouse, dating from 1838 and now containing an excellent restaurant and tavern; and Cadman's Cottage, Sydney's oldest surviving house (built in 1816). The convict-built Argyle Centre is now a complex of speciality shops and restaurants, and nearby Atherton Place is Sydney's shortest street. Restaurants and bars abound, the former catering for all tastes and all pockets, and the latter no longer rough-and-ready drinking dens but trendy pubs which often feature quite respectable evening entertainment. There are more than 80 shops, mainly in the Argyle Centre and Harrington Street, and these tend to specialise either in crafts (one shop makes beeswax candles just like those which were used in the early convict days), aboriginal art, jewellery, or the odd (one shop sells only items for the left-handed, another sells kilts). The visitors' centre has mapped out an excellent walking tour of the Rocks area, which includes all the aforementioned places plus an extension up through Argyle Cut, a road carved through the rocks by convict labour, to

New South Wales

Sydney's 'village green' and the elegant nineteenth-century homes of Millers Point. The Rocks area is an unexpected treasure to find in Sydney, or indeed in Australia, and the walking tour is well worth doing. The principal buildings are open daily.

Kings Cross, at the top of William Street, about one kilometre east of the city, has always been the Soho of Sydney, and the centre of bohemian life. Respectable enough by day, it turns on the red lights at night and becomes an area of exhibitionism, sex shops, strip joints, and slightly raffish night clubs. It is worth going just to look, for it is the only place of its kind in Australia. The discos are good, the restaurants generally poor. And beware – for the beautiful and statuesque young ladies parading the streets may not be young ladies at all. But it is safe enough, and the police keep a strict eye on it. The Kings Cross Wax Works, in the Village Centre, is worth visiting, and is open until midnight every day except Friday.

The Skywalk observation deck, on the tall Australia Square Tower in Australia Square, is an enclosed observation deck which offers a bird's-eye view of Sydney in every direction. It is open daily (except Christmas Day) until 10 p.m.

At the heart of Sydney's quite extensive Chinese quarter is the oriental-style Dixon Street, which is lined with excellent Chinese restaurants and night clubs as well as shops selling Chinese food and other goods and an art bazaar. At night, the street is lit by Chinese lanterns rather than more formal street lamps.

Paddy's market, close to Chinatown, is a Saturday market in Hay Street which sells everything from farm produce, plants and foodstuffs to clothing, live animals, crafts and bric-à-brac. It is open from 7 a.m. to 5.30 p.m.

Taronga Park Zoo, at Bradley's Head Road, Mosman, features native Australian and other exotic animals and birds, and of special interest are the rain forest aviary, the display of nocturnal creatures, and the farm animals with which children can play safely. It is open daily, and can be reached either by bus or by ferry from Circular Quay.

Besides Cadman's Cottage, which contains maritime exhibits, Sydney's principal museums are the Australian Museum in College Street, with its collection of natural history and ethnic exhibits (open daily, except Sunday and Monday mornings); the Museum of Applied Arts and Sciences, in Harris Street, Ultimo (open daily and Sunday afternoons); the Geological and Mining Museum, in George Street North (open daily and Sunday afternoons); and the Colonial

New South Wales

House Museum, in Lower Fort Street, which is a restored colonial house with authentic nineteenth-century furnishings (open daily except Christmas Day and Good Friday).

Art galleries – many of them devoted to aboriginal, other primitive, and ethnic art – abound, as do public parks. The Royal Botanic Gardens and The Domain, off Macquarie Street behind the Opera House, are two large adjoining parks which provide spectacular views of the harbour and Sydney Harbour Bridge.

Shopping in Sydney is, of course, superb. The 300-metre high Centrepoint is at the heart of the shopping area, and is surrounded by major department stores, arcades and chain stores, not to mention the multi-level shopping complex which it contains. Bounded by Market Street, Castlereagh Street, and Pitt Street, it is connected by underground and overhead covered walkways to the two largest department stores in central Sydney – David Jones and Myer. Shopping hours are from 8.30 a.m. to 5.30 p.m., except on Thursdays when there is late shopping until 9 p.m. Don't forget that all shops are closed on Saturday afternoons. Look out, too, for shopping opportunities in the MLC Centre, Australia Square, and the Royal Arcade below the Sydney Hilton. Best buy in the city is probably opal jewellery – and you are hardly likely to miss it because it is sold hard everywhere. But furs, goods from South-East Asia, and aboriginal arts and crafts are also competitively priced.

The Hilton, in Pitt Street, is a good hotel, but it is not the best in town. That honour must go to the magnificent Wentworth, which claims to be in the world's top 30 hotels but could more accurately place itself in the top ten. It is surrounded by expensive shopping arcades, has very good if expensive bars and restaurants (the Garden Court Restaurant is rather special), and possesses a rather odd coffee shop in which the customers have to clamber into facsimile railway carriages in order to eat. Such abberations apart, the Wentworth is very centrally situated in Phillip Street, and combines the most modern facilities with old-world courtesy. I like it immensely.

The Hyatt Kingsgate, at the corner of Victoria Street and Kings Cross Road, can also be recommended – it is a high-rise building with memorable views from every room. But before you run away with the idea that Sydney is a city of expensive, first-class hotels, I should add that prices are considerably lower than in Europe, and that anyway all grades of hotel, at every price, are available within the city or else on its outskirts. A list of hotels, motels, guesthouses, caravan sites and camping sites is available from the New South

New South Wales

Wales Department of Tourism or from the Sydney Visitors Bureau (291 George Street, Sydney 2000).

The range of restaurants has already been mentioned, and this again caters for every taste and every pocket. Some of the newer, ethnic restaurants are a trifle scruffy, but you will eat well in all the major hotels; in Chinatown; at the Doyle's seafood restaurants run by the extrovert Peter Doyle (there are several of these: try the one at Watson's Bay); at the Bennelong Restaurant in the Opera House; or at the Summit Restaurant, in Australia Square. The Myer Grill Brasserie, on the first floor of the Myer city store, specialises in steaks and grills. The Ensemble, at Milsons Point, is a theatre restaurant. A number of restaurants also go in for dinner-dances, among them La Taverne, in New South Head Road, Edgecliff, and The French Restaurant, in Bourke Street, Taylor Square. You will also find restaurants specialising in Japanese, Indian and Greek food, most of them first-class. See the free publication *This Week in Sydney*, available at tourist offices and in hotels.

Evening entertainment is, if anything, even more varied. Besides the attractions of the Opera House, there are seven live theatres and concerts at Sydney Town Hall. Pubs, night clubs and discos abound, and the latter are remarkably friendly places where visitors go as much for a drink and a chat with 'the natives' as for dancing, music or romance. But Sydney is also the home of a remarkable Australian phenomenon known as 'the league clubs', which are rather like social clubs in the north of England. They started out as football supporters' clubs, but today they are better known for the first-class shows and entertainment that they put on, featuring top international variety artists. Because they also serve drinks, you are supposed to be a member before going, and places are in very high demand anyway. But rules are made to be broken, and the determined tourist will usually find a place for himself for the evening. There are several of these league clubs, but the most famous is probably the St George's League Club, in Kogarah.

One cannot leave Sydney without considering the attractions which lie just outside the city centre. First of all, of course, there are its world-famous beaches. Some of these, safely shark-proofed, lie within Sydney Harbour itself, but these are small and can get very crowded at weekends or on public holidays. Bondi Beach, eight kilometres east of Sydney's city centre, is perhaps the city's best-known playground: it is too large to get really crowded, has a vast stretch of sand, is washed by the Pacific rollers, yet could hardly be

New South Wales

safer as it is netted against sharks and is patrolled by the husky, well-disciplined members of the Bondi Surf Lifesaving Club – the oldest lifesaving club in the world. It is essentially a family beach, with good changing and refreshment facilities and plenty of car-parking space, but the young and beautiful tend to go topless in its southernmost corner. Manly Beach, on the Pacific just round the northern tip of the Heads, is the other beach which is a household name worldwide, and it again is netted and patrolled and has all facilities – including some shady picnic spots. The easiest way to get to Manly is by ferry from Circular Quay: it is 15 minutes' journey away by hydrofoil or three times as long by regular ferry. Again it is essentially a family beach: if you want to take your clothes off and get an all-over tan, then the locals would prefer that you went and did it farther north at Obelisk Bay or Reef Beech, which are set aside for that purpose.

There are also one or two other things to see and do in and around Sydney which, while they may not be among the most widely recognised attractions of the city, are somehow unique.

First, anyone with an interest in architecture, or photography, would find it worthwhile to spend an hour or so wandering around the residential streets of the inner suburb of Paddington. There, many of the houses, which date from the 1890s, have balconies decorated with delicate wrought-iron work, and although the district, and the houses, fell into disrepair during and after the Second World War, the suburb is now a trendy and expensive residential area and many of the houses have been beautifully restored. The wrought-iron work, usually painted white, and known as 'Paddington lace', peeps out through mature gardens into tree-lined streets, and the overall effect is extraordinarily beautiful.

And then, perhaps, one should make a brief excursion to Vaucluse, on the road towards the southern tip of the Heads, where Vaucluse House is perhaps one of the two nearest things that Sydney has to a stately home. Vaucluse House, which is administered by a trust and is open daily, stands on the site of a large stone cottage built in 1803 by an Irish convict and nobleman, Sir Henry Brown Hayes. He called it Vaucluse after Fontaine-de-Vaucluse, in the south of France, and its idealistic setting – in beautiful grounds overlooking a tiny beach inside Sydney Harbour – caught the attention of several later purchasers, including the city's one-time Controller of Customers who was unfortunately found later to have been spending the customs dues that he collected on luxuries like Vaucluse House rather than handing them over to the government.

New South Wales

In 1827 William Charles Wentworth, the son of a surgeon and a convict woman, and one of the first white children to be born in the colony of New South Wales, bought the cottage. Wentworth, a British-educated explorer, scholar and statesman who is known as the father of the Australian Constitution, wanted the cottage because he was about to be married, and he rapidly enlarged it into the Vaucluse House that still stands today – a spacious, airy, comfortable yet imposing home built in a mixture of Georgian and Tudor Gothic styles and with an eighteenth-century style courtyard. The house, which remained in the Wentworth family until 1898, and was then allowed to fall into disrepair, has been completely restored and renovated, and is furnished with nineteenth-century antiques. Besides the house itself, outbuildings such as the stables, coach-house, bakery, laundry and guard-house can be toured, and the elegantly landscaped grounds, in which kookaburras screech disconcertingly, are a delight. You can have a snack in the adjoining tea-rooms, and the entire ambience is a pleasant contrast to the hectic bustle of nearby Sydney. The only drawback to a visit is the danger of crossing some particularly officious custodians.

Sydney's other 'stately home' is Elizabeth Bay House, a graceful Regency-style house built in 1838. It is open daily, except Mondays.

As can be seen from such contrasting attractions, Sydney is hard to describe, and even harder to sum up. The New South Wales Department of Tourism has attempted the impossible by publishing a song about the city, which is called *Australia's Leading Lady*. It goes, in part:

> She's lazy, crazy,
> Sometimes a little childish
> Busy, dizzy
> Sometimes a little wildish
> A brassy town
> Sometimes classy town
> But she's a good time
> And she'll never let you down.

Which all seems fairly accurate. But while Sydney will undoubtedly get busier and dizzier as the years go by, I don't think the song will ever really catch on.

Stretching in an arc around Sydney is the 8322 square kilometre Outer Sydney region which is made up of four distinct segments: the

New South Wales

Central Coast, to the north of Sydney; the Upper Hawkesbury district, to the northeast; the Blue Mountains, about 60 kilometres west of Sydney; and Camden-Picton, to the southwest.

The Central Coast, with its little 'capital' of Gosford, runs from the scenic Hawkesbury River, about 50 kilometres north of Sydney, to the Budgewoi and Munmorah Lakes, 70 kilometres farther north, and is a playground of mountains, forests and beaches, interspersed with farming country and orchards. Much of the farmland is former forest, but the timber was plundered for New South Wales's early shipbuilding industry.

Gosford is a pleasant little town overlooking the protected inland bay of Brisbane Water, itself part of the vast, triple-pronged Broken Bay. A couple of national parks, Ku-Ring-Gai Chae and Brisbane Water National Park, overlook Broken Bay, and the former includes a fine fauna reserve. Gosford, only just over an hour from Sydney by train, is practically a dormitory town of the state capital these days, but it is popular with holidaymakers because of its setting and because of the good range of excellent accommodation – which is not always to be taken for granted in Australia. Just outside the town a popular new tourist attraction is Old Sydney Town, an authentic re-creation of Sydney Cove and its surroundings in the days of Governor Macquarie. There are scale replicas of the cove and of many of the settlement's original buildings.

More history is to be found in the Upper Hawkesbury area, which is inland and roughly equidistant from Gosford and Sydney. The Hawkesbury River, which flows north and then east into Broken Bay, was discovered by a party led by Governor Phillip in 1789, the year after they arrived in Australia, and a short time later they returned to explore the river by boat as far as what is now the town of Richmond. In 1810 Governor Macquarie established five towns in the area – Windsor, Richmond, Castlereagh, Pitt Town and Wilberforce – and these became known as the Five Macquarie Towns. Windsor developed into the administrative centre of the region, with its own government house, court house, gaol and barracks, and many old buildings remain – among them the restored Court House, Greenway's fine St Matthew's Church, an inn now housing the Hawkesbury Museum, and the colonial terraced house known as The Doctor's House. Richmond contains the stately Hobartville, a Georgian property; and at Wilberforce the Australiana Village (open daily) is a memorial to the pioneering days.

New South Wales

The Blue Mountains are a spectacular region of mountains and valleys astride the Great Western Highway leading to the fertile western part of New South Wales. Much of the region is a national park, and the precipitous cliffs, fern-filled gorges and ravines are not only the haunt of a variety of wildlife but also offer some of the best bush-walking in Australia. Typical of these walks are the 6-kilometre long, 2½-hour Federal Pass Walk, which takes in the Leura Falls and the 245-metre high Katoomba Falls, and includes a (fortunately) downhill flight of 1330 steps; the Grand Canyon and Rodriguez Pass Walks, at Blackheath; the National Pass Walk at Wentworth Falls and Minnehahah Falls; and the Prince Henry Cliff Walk and Federal Pass Walk at Katoomba. Katoomba, 104 kilometres from Sydney, is a popular summer resort with a great variety of all sorts of accommodation, a scenic railway which with a gradient of one in two is said to be the steepest in the world, the Scenic Skyway aerial cable-car ride over Cookes Crossing, and easy accessibility to the Jenolan Caves. The rotating Skyway Restaurant, at the Scenic Skyway and scenic railway terminus, provides diners with some awesome views over the surrounding countryside, including the Katoomba Falls, the much-photographed triple-pronged sandstone formation known as the Three Sisters, and the Jamieson Valley. Other places of interest include the Wirrimburra Flora and Fauna Sanctuary, the Greens Motorcade Museum, the Rail Transport Museum, and the Warragamba Dam. The Norman Lindsay Gallery and Museum at Springwood is the former home of veteran Australian artist Norman Lindsay, and is set in attractive bushland and formal gardens. There are more gardens to see at Leura, where the National Trust has its ornamental gardens, Everglades. And it is worth remembering that the whole Blue Mountains region is within easy day-trip reach of Sydney.

The Camden-Picton district is farming country, and was first settled by European farmers on the recommendation of helpful aboriginals. There is a popular attraction on the road to Camden in the shape of El Caballo Blanco, a Spanish-style hacienda at Catherine Field where the famous Andalusian dancing horses give displays. The Camden Museum of Aviation, at Narellan, is also of considerable interest. Picton, 80 kilometres from Sydney, is a peculiarly English little town, complete with railway viaduct. Local beauty spots include the Burragorang Lookout, from which there are panoramic views, and the districts several dams which

New South Wales

provide Sydney's water. Flora and fauna sanctuaries, a lion park, and a smattering of wineries complete the region's attractions.

Most wine enthusiasts, however, will head beyond the Outer Sydney region to the Hunter Valley, 160 kilometres northwest of Sydney. The Hunter region as a whole is known for its fine dairy-farming, cereal farming, and even bloodstock rearing. But it is for its wines that it is best known – indeed, some say that it produces the best wine in Australia (although South Australia's Barossa Valley would disagree with that, and I might support their view). Grapes were first grown in the Hunter Valley in the 1830s, and today the wine compares well with better-known overseas competitors and, in Australia at any rate, costs a fraction of the price. Most Hunter Valley wineries welcome visitors, and besides demonstrating how the wine is produced they usually offer liberal tastings.

The region as a whole is full of contrasts. Hunter Valley itself is prone to floods and droughts; there are rich seams of coal beneath it, some of which are being mined; yet at places like Barrington Tops one is in thickly wooded country popular with riders, anglers and walkers. The contrast is underlined by the presence, at the mouth of the Hunter River, of New South Wales's second city: Newcastle. Like its British namesake, Newcastle is an industrial giant of a city, founded on steel, yet it has attractive beaches right next to the smelters. But I don't see it as a tourist town – and, indeed, the next 500 to 600 kilometres of coastline, leading all the way up to Tweed Heads and the Queensland border, probably do not see many overseas tourists either, although there are a number of places of interest on the way.

Port Stephens, 48 kilometres north of Newcastle, is a game fishing centre, and there are more water sports to be found on and around Lake Macquarie, the largest seaboard lake in Australia. Farther north still, the coastline and the climate begin to get a rather more tropical feel about them, and the region – known as the Holiday Coast – really could do with a few more overseas visitors. Australians know it as an endless stretch of golden beaches ideal for surfing, swimming, fishing or simply sunbathing – and never crowded. The principal resorts are Port Macquarie (where the patrolled Flynn's Beach is excellent for surfing), Nambucca Harbour, Coffs Harbour (where the Bruxner Park Flora Reserve and the Kumbaingeri Wildlife Sanctuary are an added attraction), and the 'garden city' of Grafton, which lies inland and stages an annual Jacaranda Festival

New South Wales

in the first week of November. There are any number of smaller resorts along this coast, and some dramatic features too – including the 1157-metre high Mount Warning, in its own national park overlooking the attractive Tweed Valley and close to some particularly delightful rolling green farmland; the spectacular view from Cape Byron lighthouse; and the dramatic Dorrigo National Park. Although this stretch of coastline, stretching up to the Queensland border, is popular with holidaymaking Australians and is described in official brochures as having 'big city amenities', it is important to stress that in European terms the coastline has hardly been developed at all – and the hinterland is absolutely charming. The amenities are there, by and large, but the crowds definitely are not. I think this 'border' region would be one of the best areas in the whole of Australia in which to take a self-drive motoring holiday, but because of the distances involved it should be based in Brisbane (see Chapter 10) rather than Sydney.

Inland from the Holiday Coast is the New England region, where the wheatfields, pastureland and river fishing may be English-style but the sprawling mountains of the Great Dividing Range and the occasional cotton fields most definitely are not. It is beloved by bush walkers, climbers, and motorists, as well as by people who enjoy – sometimes successfully – 'fossicking' for diamonds, sapphires, topaz, garnets and zircons. The university city of Armidale has good road and rail links with Sydney, 566 kilometres to the south, and Tenterfield is another gem 'fossicking' centre close to mineral-rich Inverell and the mountain town of Glen Innes. Tamworth is the country music capital of Australia, a sort of Nashville, Tennessee, in miniature, where the annual Australian Country Music awards are contested.

There is equally varied and memorable scenery to be found to the south of Sydney, with fine fishing on the Pacific coast and inland a collection of fauna reserves, rain forests, waterfalls, lakes and rivers. Wollongong, a thriving industrial city and seaport, is 92 kilometres south of Sydney, and the surrounding region is again rich in mementoes of the state's earliest days of exploration and settlement. These days can be relived by visiting the Illawarra Historical Museum.

Open farmland and rugged timber-clad ranges typify the Southern Highlands which, at 600 to 750 metres above sea level are not particularly high except in relation to their surroundings. Tourists can overnight in towns like Goulburn, Bowral and Berrima. The

5 Como Mansion, Melbourne: one of Australia's oldest stately homes.

6 Southern panorama: the Tasman Bridge, Hobart, Tasmania.

7 Australian seascape: the tesselated pavement and Eaglehawk Neck, Tasmania.

8 Ayers Rock, in central Australia, turns blood-red at sunset.

New South Wales

Wombeyan Caves, near Mittagong, are famous for their strange and delicate limestone formations.

Trains from Sydney travel down as far as Nowra, 160 kilometres from Sydney, and en route passengers pass seemingly endless Pacific beaches of golden sand and rolling surf. Stop, and you can choose a beach all to yourself. From Nowra, Highway 1 – the romantic road which practically circles Australia – winds on through small country towns, beach resorts and national parks. Merimbula, which is connected with Sydney by air, would be a good centre in which to hire a car and do a little exploring.

West of Sydney, on the far side of the Blue Mountains, lie the rich wheatlands and sheep-farming country which ensured that the original settlers in New South Wales had, once they had crossed the Blue Mountains, come to stay. The principal town is Bathurst, 209 kilometres from Sydney, which won fame as the centre of the New South Wales gold rush. There's living history at the Lachlan Vintage Village; and the once-volcanic terrain of the Wurrumbungle National Park, near Coonabarabran, is rich in wildlife. The Siding Spring Astronomy Exhibition can also be visited from Coonabarabran.

The dairy farms, orchards, sheep farms, vineyards, wheatfields and ricefields spread right across southwestern New South Wales, irrigated by the Murray and Murrumbidgee Rivers, Australia's major river system. Riverboat holidays are a popular, and rather 'different' attraction in this region, but might be best taken from South Australia (see Chapter 8). Important towns and cities are Wagga Wagga, on the Murrumbidgee; Albury, on the Murray; Deniliquin; the wheat town of Narrandera; Griffith; and Leeton. Wineries (around Albury and Griffith) make visitors more than welcome, while sheep farms and irrigation schemes can also be toured.

But if this region suggests that New South Wales is principally a farming state, then journey on – to the far west. You will find yourself in the outback, where the 'town' marked on your map may prove to be simply a tiny settlement or a single farm, and where they measure the sheep stations in square miles rather than acres. And out there, sitting on enormous mineral deposits, are towns like Lightning Ridge (where the world's only known deposits of black opal have been found) and the 'silver city' of Broken Hill. Lead, zinc, copper and gemstones have all been found in Broken Hill, as well as the now almost exhausted silver deposits. It's hardly a tourist resort, even

New South Wales

though it does have road and rail links with Sydney. It is, significantly, a base for the Royal Flying Doctor Service and the School of the Air (see also Chapter 11). For beyond it, and indeed around it, there is an awful lot of nothing.

7 Victoria

Victoria, in the southeastern corner of Australia, is – the Australian Capital Territory excepted – the smallest state in Australia and is aptly named. It is the most British of the states, and in many ways it is quaintly old-fashioned when compared to the rest of the country. The businessman of Melbourne, its capital, go about their work dressed in dark suits, and collars and ties – an oddity in a country where shorts are acceptable formal wear in the summer months and where, in country areas, you may even find officialdom with its bare feet thrust into skimpy sandals. Melbourne is Victorian in ambience (it is often described, with some accuracy, as the best-preserved Victorian city in the world), and also in atmosphere. Sometimes its morals are Victorian, too – the Victorian painting of a nude, familiarly known as Chloe, in the famous Young and Jackson's pub opposite Melbourne's main Flinders Street station has twice been slashed by customers who apparently object to the undertones of moral laxity which a casual observer might be forgiven for thinking epitomised – rather than offended against – the mores of modern Australia.

That Melbourne, and the state of Victoria, are there at all, however, is due to a distincly immoral act on the part of explorers and sheep farmers from Tasmania (then called Van Dieman's Land) who, in the early part of the nineteenth century, crossed the Bass Strait and began to settle the rich pastoral land around Port Phillip Bay in direct contradiction of orders from the governor of Sydney that anyone settling in an area beyond a 300-kilometre ring around Sydney was a trespasser and would not be protected by the law.

The newcomers, led by John Batman, formed a group known as 'The Port Phillip Association', bought the 700,000 acres of land that they were farming from the aborigines in return for blankets and knives, christened their settlement Bearbrass, and invited the governor to visit them. This visit, in 1837, put the stamp of legality on Bearbrass and in return the settlers agreed to the governor's suggestions that their town should be renamed Melbourne, after the then British prime minister, and that some slight modifications should be made to the grid layout of the embryonic city.

The Port Phillip Bay region grew rapidly, the newly named Melbourne developed into a bustling, if not particularly attractive, port, and in 1851 Victoria was granted its independence. Its flow of settlers, however, was immediately interrupted by the discovery of gold in New South Wales. Alarmed by the rapid disappearance of its population, the fledgling state of Victoria launched its own hunt for gold, and within days rich seams of the precious metal had been discovered at Ballarat and Bendigo, both close to the capital. The great Australian gold rush was on, and neither Victoria nor Melbourne ever looked back. Indeed, Melbourne was to grow into a major city which, by the turn of the century, was challenging Sydney as the prospective capital of a unified, federated, Australia – a rivalry which led directly to the setting up of Canberra as a purpose-built national capital, but which mutters on to this day and is reflected especially in a determination in Melbourne to be different to Sydney, and vice versa. Cricket matches between New South Wales and Victoria, played either in Sydney or at the beautiful and historic Melbourne Cricket Ground, are still momentous occasions which engender as much rivalry as – often more than – an international Test match.

Indeed, one could almost start a tour of Melbourne with a look at MCG, as the cricket ground is universally known, for not only does it reflect the Victorians' love of – one might almost say 'obsession with' – outdoor sports, but it is an historic spot in its own right: it was the setting for the 1956 Olympic Games; and the world record cricket crowd, 90,000 people, watched a Test match there in 1961 (there have been even larger crowds at MCG for the finals of Australian Rules Football – Australia's other major spectator sport). After the matches, cricket players and personalities often go for a drink in the Cricketers' Bar of the Hilton Hotel, opposite MCG, there to be either lauded or ignored, depending on how well, or how badly, they and the team have performed. If you want to be a hero in Australia, you have to work at it! The Hilton stands on the site of Clifton Mansions which, according to a plaque inside the hotel commemorating the centenary of Australia versus England Test matches (1877–1977) is 'where the Ashes were created'. This is a somewhat mysterious claim: the Ashes, the mythical trophy for which the Australian and England teams play, are popularly supposed to be the ashes of the bails used in the England versus Australia Test of 1882, when Australia beat England for the first time. But that match was played in England, and according to official record books the term 'the Ashes' derives from a headline in *The Sporting Times* in 1882 reporting England's defeat and referring to 'the ashes of English cricket'.

That profligate claim apart, Melbourne is a conservative city. Its wealth of Victorian buildings are now being carefully preserved, and in some cases restored, and the old blends pleasantly with the new.

You can ride around the town on its rumbling single-decker trams (which serve a dual role in that they provide public transport but at the same time successfully slow down more modern traffic to such a degree that many motorists strive to avoid the city centre, leaving the streets pleasantly uncrowded), or you can take the new underground suburban 'loop' line which links the city centre with the outlying suburbs spread along the golden coastline and stretching into the rolling farmland of the interior. The suburban rail services from the recently restored Renaissance-style Flinders Street station in the city centre are frequent and excellent, if not particularly rapid, and the station – complete with copper dome and two clock towers – is the busiest in the world during the morning and evening rush hours.

The docks are scruffy, but then what docks (Sydney apart) are not? And at least a lot of very good work has been done on cleaning up the Yarra River, which flows sluggishly through the centre of the city. A lot of unkind things have been said and written about the Yarra. It is muddy in appearance, and local people refer to it slightingly as 'the river which flows upside-down'. But the 'mud' is silt, and both the water and the landscaped river banks have been cleaned up and beautified in recent years – partly as a result of incessant prodding from the lively daily newspaper, *The Melbourne Age*, which ran a tireless campaign under the very Australian slogan: 'Give the Yarra a Go'. Melbourne has indeed 'given the Yarra a go' – thereby adding greatly to the attraction of smart riverside suburbs like Toorak, where most of the foreign embassies were located until they were compulsorily relocated in Canberra in 1955.

Other inner suburbs are getting a facelift, too. Many of them consist largely of small Victorian or Edwardian houses with wrought-iron latticework balconies, and these properties fell into disrepair in the immediate post-war years and the inner suburbs became virtually slum areas. But as property values fell and

Victoria

transport costs rose, these houses were 'rediscovered' and bought up, particularly by younger residents, and most of the properties have now been restored to their former grace. The owners' hard work has paid off: these houses are now much sought-after and are very costly.

There are excellent half-day and whole-day coach tours of Melbourne operated by firms like Australian Pacific Tours (details from APT or from the Victorian Government Travel Centre, 230 Collins Street), and typically one of these would include such major city attractions as the beautifully landscaped Royal Botanic Gardens (admission free); Captain Cook's Cottage; the Old Gaol; and the Shrine of Remembrance.

Melbourne is a city of many parks, and the Royal Botanic Gardens, in Domain Gardens, is the most attractive of these. Situated between Alexander Avenue and Domain Road, they consist of 88 acres of classically landscaped gardens – more than half of this space being given over to flower beds – and three artificial lakes. The gardens are popular for lunchtime and evening strolls, and in respect of the latter it is important to add that the streets (and parks) of Melbourne are completely safe at all times. Mugging and vandalism are urban vices still virtually unknown in Australia.

The city's major park is the King's Domain, lying between the Royal Botanic Gardens and the city. It contains the restored La Trobe's Cottage, once the residence of Victoria's first lieutenant-governor and thus Victoria's first Government House (open daily), and the modern Sydney Myer Music Bowl, where free outdoor concerts are staged on summer evenings. In Royal Park, Melbourne has a pleasant little zoo which is well stocked with indigenous Australian birds and mammals.

Captain Cook's Cottage, the family home of the 'discoverer' of Australia, is a major Australian landmark, and stands in another park, Fitzroy Gardens, just down the road from the triple Gothic spires of the Roman Catholic cathedral of St Patrick – irreverently known locally as 'St Pat's'. This really is a little corner of olde Englande, with the brick cottage standing under spreading trees and among startlingly colourful flowerbeds – the work of Melbourne City Council's apparently tireless Parks and Recreation Department, which also keeps a display of hot-house plants in an adjoining conservatory. And if the cottage seems a little out of place in the heart of Melbourne, or even in Australia . . . then it is. It was shipped out from Yorkshire brick by brick – even though it seems extremely doubtful whether Cook ever lived there, as it was built by his parents long after the explorer had begun his travels. There are conducted tours of the cottage (which does contain a cabin trunk bearing Cook's initials), but only a few people can be admitted at any one time because it is so tiny.

The Old Gaol, opposite the present-day police headquarters in Russell Street, is a National Trust property of morbid interest to the worshippers of Australian folk heroes. Built in 1841, it was the scene of the execution of one of the country's most famous 'bushrangers' (i.e. outlaws), Ned Kelly. Open daily, the Old Gaol contains a small penal museum in which can be seen the scaffold from which Kelly was hanged, and a suit of armour which he built for himself out of scrap metal. Oddly, for such an historic building, part of it is used as a garage.

The Shrine of Remembrance, next to the Royal Botanic Gardens in King's Domain, is an impressive memorial to Victoria's war dead, built in the massive style which former British colonies seem to espouse and which Britain herself has never equalled. A single soldier, wearing the familiar slouch hat of Australian troops in the Second World War, guards this beautiful and evocative building, with its steep steps leading up to the shrine's main hall with its central plaque – or Rock of Remembrance – bearing the familiar, if incomplete, quotation: 'Greater love hath no man'. The skylights of the shrine have been built so that at the 11th hour of the 11th day of the 11th month – the moment of the Armistice which ended the First World War – a ray of sunlight strikes the word 'love' on the Rock of Remembrance. Steps inside the shrine lead up to balconies from which there are panoramic views of Melbourne's skyline with the parks and the Yarra River in the foreground.

Just below the Shrine of Remembrance, and also in King's Domain, is Government House, the white tower of which can be seen from almost all over the central part of the city. It is almost a symbol of the city . . . almost, but not quite. Also almost a symbol is the peculiar chrome spire of the Arts Centre in St Kilda Road, which leads from King's Domain down to Flinders Street station. The Arts Centre contains the state's art gallery, in which are housed a number of famous Australian paintings. But it is as remarkable for its architecture as its contents: the roadside fountains are backed by entrance doors which appear to be made of (and actually contain) running water.

Victoria

Another spot in the city which might be thought to symbolise it, but doesn't, is City Square, and the junctions of Collins Street, Regent Place, Flinders Lane and Swanston Street. Seen by the city as one of its most important structural projects ever, designed as a visual link between two of its major buildings (the Town Hall and St Paul's Cathedral), and opened by the Queen in 1980, City Square has seating for thousands of people, including 350 in a glass-roofed amphitheatre. Fountains, shops, restaurants, live entertainment – the square has them all, and does genuinely serve as a focal point for the entertainment and cultural life of the city (including open-air concerts in the square). But it is still not *quite* what Melbourne is looking for.

The problem, of course, is that Sydney has had its Harbour Bridge for half a century, and now has its Opera House as well, and both symbolise Sydney as conclusively as the Eiffel Tower symbolises Paris. But what can be said to symbolise Melbourne? The city fathers, and not a few of its residents, are getting quite neurotic trying to find an answer to that.

They have even offered a hefty prize for the person who comes up with the definitive answer. Which is a pity, because the answer is right in front of their noses.

There are other Victorian cities in the world, and there are other garden cities too. But the combination of the two is unique. It is what gives Melbourne its atmosphere and its character: two things which are far more important than any man-made monstrosity built, apparently, for the sole purpose of 'putting one over' on Sydney.

Melbourne is on the banks of the Yarra, infested with daytime joggers and dotted with free barbecue stands for weekend picnickers. It is the oleander-lined streets of Toorak Village, the suburb which is just about as villagey as Hollywood and almost as expensive (a house there could cost you $A1 million – but for that money you can be choosy, and even pick an oddly out-of-place English-style, half-timbered home if you wish). It is the glaring white façade of the National Trust's classically colonial mansion of Como, in South Yarra, with its verandahs, and ironwork, and period furniture, and cool green gardens. It is Swan Street Bridge, which crosses the Yarra below Como and affords unexpectedly good views of the city centre. It is the trams. And above all it is that city centre itself, a city centre which sometimes seems to have been built in homage to the British queen after whom the state of

Victoria was named. Her landmarks are everywhere: Victoria Street, the Queen Victoria Medical Centre, Queen Victoria Gardens . . . the list is endless.

And lots of the old buildings, scattered in almost haphazard fashion around the city, are fascinating in their own right. The Victorian inhabitants of old Melbourne were, one suspects, rather nice people. They were fiercely patriotic, and fiercely loyal to the British crown. They wanted to do things correctly. They worked hard, and when they had earned their money they splashed it around a bit.

The centre of their world was Spring Street. There, at the top of Bourke Street, stands the neo-classic State Parliament House, which was begun in 1856 and still lacks the north and south wings and dome included in the original plans. The federal parliament met there from 1901 to 1927, but today only Victoria's state legislature meets behind its Doric columns. There are guided tours of the building every weekday.

Also in Spring Street are the elaborately decorated Princess Theatre, built in 1887 to mark Queen Victoria's silver jubilee and still going strong, and the Old Treasury Building, which today houses state government offices. Although built in Renaissance style, the Old Treasury Building, which looks down the length of Collins Street, is another piece of Victoriana, for it was constructed between 1859 and 1862. At the time of the gold rush it was a busy place, and its vaults have held up to 100 million pounds worth of gold from the Victorian goldfields in their day. Now, besides fulfilling its governmental role, the building is cared for by the National Trust; and its tan-coloured plaster exterior, fringed with maroon paint on the window frames, intrudes oddly – if architecturally accurately – into the solidly Victorian surroundings.

The Hotel Windsor, opposite, is a magnificent old hotel. It too has its place in the history of Victorian Melbourne, for it was originally built to accommodate out-of-town gold prospectors who, at weekends, would come into Melbourne with their wives and families, dressed in their Sunday best, to spend their new-found wealth. One likes to imagine that the menfolk might also have gone for a drink at the old White Hart pub on the corner – now the Imperial Hotel.

For a bird's-eye view of Melbourne, visitors can go to the observation deck of the National Mutual building, at the corner of Williams Street and Collins Street, or the 21st floor of the ICI

Victoria

Building in Nicholson Street. Both are open on weekdays. They are the face of the modern Melbourne, as is the new, American-style Wentworth Hotel, with its shopping arcades and bubble lifts.

Besides the Wentworth – which is an excellent, top-class hotel without coming up to the standards of its namesake in Sydney – other good hotels in Melbourne are the Southern Cross (the city's first international hotel, which also includes a shopping complex), the Sheraton, Noah's, the Chateau Commodore, the Victoria, and the aforementioned Hilton. The principal hotels, and Flinders Street station, are linked with Melbourne's international Tullamarine Airport by a half-hourly shuttle bus, which takes 20 to 30 minutes for the trip and for which the fare is about one-third of the equivalent journey by taxi. Bus pick-ups can be arranged by telephoning 347 8238.

The main shopping areas are in Collins Street, Bourke Street and Lonsdale Street, although there are also some very pleasant arcades such as Royal Arcade. The Myer department store, between Elizabeth Street and Swanston Street, is the largest shop of its kind in the southern hemisphere. Georges, in Collins Street, is probably the most exclusive store in town; it stands next door to the fine Presbyterian church known as The Scott's Church. For shoppers, fashion (very up-to-date) and household goods are the best buys, although there is a full range of Australian souvenirs, plus native goods from New Guinea. Shops generally stay open late on Friday evenings, and close for the weekend at lunchtime on Saturday.

Evening entertainments are a trifle sparse, although there are concerts at the Victorian Arts Centre and the Sydney Myer Music Bowl, as well as other venues mentioned earlier. The locals seem to prefer eating out, and a few go on to discos like the one at the Hilton (rather poor). They also conserve their energies for sporting activities, and for celebrations like Melbourne Cup week (early November), the Australian Rules Football finals at MCG (late September), and the Moomba Festival (March) – all occasions during which it is very hard to find accommodation in the city.

Outside the principal hotels, good restaurants are surprisingly few and far between, too. One very pleasant BYOG restaurant is Donlevy's, in Middle Park, close to the city centre, which has Continental-style cuisine and is remarkably cheap. Rather better known are the expensive French restaurant, Fanny's; the Italian-style Florentino Restaurant; Lazar's, which with its antique furnishings and silver cutlery is perhaps what one might expect of

Victoria

Melbourne; and Pamplemousse, another French-style restaurant with live music and dancing. Hotel restaurants tend to be pricey. Inexpensive, but fun in the evenings, is the Green House Restaurant, opposite the Royal Botanic Gardens – it is built to resemble the inside of a greenhouse, and it is popular for business lunches, too. Government travel centres issue a useful free leaflet called *Dining Out in Melbourne* if you wish to investigate further before choosing where to eat. As for what to eat, local specialities include the whiting and most varieties of shellfish, and ethnic restaurants (and dishes) are always sought after.

Within easy reach, by tram or train, of the city centre are the inner suburbs mentioned earlier, many of which have distinctive nineteenth-century architecture (Carlton, South Melbourne, Fitzroy and Parkville are particularly rich in Victorian terraced houses situated along tree-lined streets or around elegant squares). As with most British and European cities, the houses get more modern the farther you get out of town, and in Melbourne this is particularly noticeable as one travels by suburban railway train east, around the coast of Port Phillip Bay. A string of modern seaside suburbs follows one after the other, and one would imagine that most of these – wealthy-looking, self-contained centres only an hour from Flinders Street station – would be very pleasant to live in indeed. Port Phillip Bay, 61 kilometres long and just as wide, with Melbourne at the head of it and the coastline beyond, lend themselves to this particularly attractive, if somewhat uncontrolled, kind of urban sprawl.

East of Port Phillip Bay is another almost circular bay, Westernport Bay, which has French Island at its centre and Phillip Island at its mouth. The latter is famous for an extraordinary spectacle which takes place there every evening, when thousands of fairy penguins – less than a foot (30 centimetres) tall – waddle out of the sea, where they have spent the day feeding, and back to their burrows in the sand-dunes. The spectacle is known as the Penguin Parade. There are holiday cottages on the island, which also has vast numbers of other bird species – including pelicans, egrets, ibis, herons and spoonbills – as well as seals and a colony of koala bears.

From Westernport Bay, the coastline dips south to another popular tourist spot, Wilson's Promontory, known to Australians as 'the Prom'. This mountainous peninsula, 223 kilometres southeast of Melbourne, is preserved as a national park and is rich in flora and fauna including wallabies and wombats. The Prom is a popular place for caravanners and campers.

Victoria

East of the Prom stretches the 145-kilometre long Ninety Mile Beach, a largely unspoilt coastline popular with surfers and fishermen. Inland from the beach are the Gippsland Lakes, another holiday playground consisting of 80 kilometres of interconnected lakes running parallel to the shore and ideal for boating and cruising holidays (vessels can be booked through the Victorian Government Travel Centre in Melbourne).

There are more superb beaches to the southwest of Melbourne, within easy reach of Geelong, Victoria's second city and 72 kilometres from the capital. Good roads and rail services connect Melbourne with Geelong, a wool-trading centre and port which has a lot of parkland and a good range of hotel accommodation as well as extensive camping and caravanning facilities.

Geelong is on the western tip of Port Phillip Bay, and the adjoining Bellarine Peninsula houses several attractive holiday areas with facilities ranging from sheltered bay boating to ocean surfing. Again, there is a good choice of both hotel accommodation and camping facilities – as, indeed, there is all along this coastline.

The coastline can be followed on the 300-kilometre long Great Ocean Road, which runs from Torquay, just south of Geelong, to Warrnambool. There are a number of small resorts along the way, most of them devoted to outdoor sports. But watch out for unexpected hazards: like the kangaroos which graze on the greens of the golf course at Anglesea. The western part of the Great Ocean Road, west of Port Campbell, runs through the Port Campbell National Park, a particularly spectacular 30-kilometre stretch of coastline along which the cliffs have been eroded into natural arches and pillars. Visitors from Melbourne or Geelong taking this very attractive route, however, have no need to retrace their steps on the return journey: at Warrnambool they can pick up Highway 1 and take the inland route back to either town.

Northeast of Melbourne, and unexpectedly close to the city itself, are the pleasant and colourful hills and valleys of the Dandenong Ranges – with Ferntree Gully National Park (where you might just see a duck-billed platypus in the wild) and Sherbrooke Forest (one of the best places in Australia to see lyrebirds) as the pick of their various tourist attractions.

Visitors can also see the duck-billed platypus, this time in captivity, in the Healesville Sanctuary, just north of the Dandenongs. The sanctuary was the first place in which the shy, nervous and elusive platypus was bred in captivity. Healesville, a resort

Victoria

town, is in the foothills of the Great Dividing Range, and nearby Mount Donna Buang is the closest ski resort to Melbourne. For like New South Wales, Victoria does have its snowfields, most of them in the Southern Alps. The terrain is gentle, and powder snow is rare, so cross-country skiing is often preferred to the downhill variety, but the major ski resorts are Mount Buller, Mount Buffalo, Mount Hotham and Falls Creek, all northeast of Melbourne and between 240 and 380 kilometres from the city.

Northwest of Melbourne, the pasture lands eventually give way to more mountains: the eroded red sandstone of the Grampians, which are also on the edge of the Great Dividing Range. The Grampians – with such oddly shaped features as Mushroom Rock and the Lady's Hat – are magnificent hiking country, and are again rich in wildlife of all kinds. Some of the caves in the Grampians contain aboriginal rock paintings.

There are a number of big sheep stations northwest of Melbourne and some, such as Naringal, near Cape Clear, welcome visitors. There, one can watch shepherding and sheep-shearing – and even join in. Naringal is one station which actually accommodates guests. But if sheep-shearing is one of the famous activities associated with the state of Victoria, it cannot match panning for gold. You can do that in Ballarat – and if you are lucky enough, or skilled enough, or both, you just might strike it rich and recover the cost of your holiday.

Ballarat and Bendigo – both within easy reach of Melbourne – were the two original gold-mining towns of Victoria. Between them, in the years following the gold rush of 1851, they produced more gold than all the Californian goldfields put together. And, although the gold is long gone, both towns still have an air of solid prosperity about them.

Bendigo, 153 kilometres from Melbourne, is a wealthy agricultural and sheep-farming centre with some particularly fine examples of Victorian architecture among its buildings – including the town hall, the law courts, two churches, the post office, the old police barracks, and the Fortuna Villa mansion. The Central Deborah gold mine has been restored to its original working condition, and there are interesting tours of it daily.

Bendigo has survived because it ploughed some of its wealth back into the town, and because of its agricultural interests. Ballarat, too, has survived because it developed other industries such as engineering. But lots of gold rush towns were not so lucky. When the gold ran

Victoria

out, the populations vanished as quickly as they had appeared, and only 'ghost towns' – an unexpected discovery in a country as new as Australia – were left behind. On the road from Melbourne to Ballarat after driving through the 'new town' of Melton which is being developed to deal with the overspill of Melbourne's population, which has already passed 2·7 million, you pass one of these ghost towns, and the contrast between it and Melton is dramatic. It is just a collection of dilapidated timber buildings now, but its ups and downs over the past century or so would have been remarkable: up when the gold prospectors passed through it on their way to and from the mines at Ballarat; down when the gold rush ended; up again when it became a vital link on the telephone lines to Melbourne; down again when subscriber trunk dialling was introduced into Australia's telephone system; and finally 'out' when the road was straightened and turned into a dual carriageway, and the settlement was bypassed altogether.

Ballarat, 113 kilometres from Melbourne, is a very attractive town full of parks, gardens, churches, Victorian buildings – and full of interest too. Besides the goldfields, its main claim to fame is that it was the scene of Australia's only civil war: the Eureka Stockade rebellion in 1854. Although the war lasted only 13 minutes, it cost the lives of 28 men, and many more were wounded. The Stockade itself has now been recreated beside a memorial to the incident, and a brief sound-and-light performance in an adjoining hut tells the story of what happened.

Gold prospecting was not as straightforward as it sounds, for there was annoying bureaucracy even in 1854. Technically, the crown owned the land which was being prospected, and although prospectors were allowed to keep any gold they found they did have to buy licences which cost £1.50 a month. Prospectors who did not have these licences – and most could not afford them until they had actually struck gold – were pestered by the police and corrupt officials, and finally a group of 150 diggers led by Peter Lawler declared themselves independent and manned a wooden stockade.

The stockade was manned on 29 November. At 4 a.m. on 3 December, a Sunday, it was stormed by 400 soldiers and armed police who indiscriminately attacked anyone in sight – bayoneting the wounded and sabring onlookers. Twenty-two miners and onlookers were killed, against the attackers' casualties of six soldiers dead and one policeman wounded.

Lawler, who lost an arm, was smuggled away by the sympathetic townsfolk. Thirteen of his fellows were accused of high treason and

Victoria

faced the death penalty, but were acquitted by the courts amid great popular rejoicing. And sweeping reforms in the laws governing gold prospecting and the licensing of the diggers were to follow. The miners might be thought to have made their point, albeit at appalling cost, but words on the Stockade Memorial show a certain degree of fence-sitting by the authorities. They refer, tactfully at least, to 'the heroic pioneers who fought and fell on this sacred spot in the cause of liberty, and the soldiers who fell at Duty's call'.

The nearby Botanic Gardens are as colourful and well-kept as any in Australia, and contain the Begonia House which is the centrepiece of the town's annual Begonia Festival in March. Indeed this is a town full of flowers – for even the central strips of the main roads, once plied by somewhat unstable trams with short wheelbases and known locally as 'Leaping Lizzies', have been converted into endless rose beds. In the Botanic Gardens themselves, a popular feature is an avenue of busts of all Australia's premiers, peeping shyly around and through masses of flowering trees and shrubs.

Besides the Botanic Gardens and the Stockade, Ballarat's principal tourist attraction is Sovereign Hill, a fascinating re-creation of a gold-mining township of the 1850s. Authentically designed shops, houses and other buildings line the streets of the township, and local volunteers in period costume staff the shops and walk the streets acting as guides. At the diggings, visitors can see how the prospectors lived and worked, and in Red Hill Gully Creek you can even try your hand at a little gold-panning, a time-consuming occupation which is much harder than it looks, but which might just pay off if you stick at it. There are underground tours of the diggings, which were sunk by miners when the easy surface pickings ran out, and a mining museum shows the later developments of company mining.

The shops, bakeries, pubs and so on are like those in American re-creations of Wild West towns: not just models, but flourishing little businesses in their own right in what can only be described as a living museum. One could happily spend a day at Sovereign Hill: a day which should prove to be both educational and fun. You can tour the township in a horse-drawn Cobb and Company coach, have lunch or tea in the New York Bakery, or dine in style at the United States Hotel which has an excellent and wide-ranging menu and where a good meal costs what it would in a fairly bargain-priced Melbourne restaurant. The United States Hotel doubles up as the township's bar as well – but watch out for the patrolling constable, swinging his truncheon absent-mindedly, who feels free to question

Victoria

all visitors as to their identity and reasons for visiting Sovereign Hill, and who has been known to handcuff noisy revellers until they cool off. Talk to him nicely, or buy him a drink, however, and he may reveal his British ancestry!

Opposite Sovereign Hill is Ballarat's Gold Museum, which tells the story of gold and the part that it has played in man's history. Exhibits include the use to which gold was put by ancient civilisations, gold coins from all over the world, the history of the gold rush and Australian coinage, and the scientific uses of gold today.

Less easily reached from Melbourne than fascinating Ballarat is the northeastern border country of Victoria, bounded by the Murray River. But one can drive alongside the river on the Murray River Highway, or travel it by boat (there are cruises from Echuca, Swan Hill and Mildura). Once southeastern Australia's main highway, the Murray River is dotted with small river towns and ports, formerly vital trade centres linked by huge fleets of paddle steamers. The three ports mentioned above are probably the most attractive, and are full of historic interest. One historic item in Mildura is peculiarly Australian: it is the claimant to the title of the longest bar in the world. You'll find it in the Mildura Working Men's Club – and it measures a formidable 87 metres.

8 South Australia

South Australia is a strange state. It modestly, and accurately, describes itself as the poor relation of the other states, and with a population of only 1·2 million (of whom one million live in or around the capital of Adelaide) it certainly has a struggle to make ends meet financially, because of the small tax base. Its portion of the main road north to Alice Springs, in the centre of Australia, for example, is an unsealed dirt road for much of its route across South Australia –while the Northern Territory, with vast national government funds to fall back on, long ago sealed its even more remote portion of the trans-continental road from Alice Springs to the northern coastal territorial capital of Darwin.

As far as tourism is concerned, South Australia is also slightly off the beaten track – at least in theory. Yet European visitors flock there because Adelaide is, after Melbourne, the most British of Australian cities, and the state is even now going through the process of turning Adelaide airport into an international airport with direct links to Europe and the Far East. And one suspects that first-time visitors to the state, who perhaps go there largely because they are visiting friends, or relatives, get a pleasant surprise. Adelaide, with its peaceful linear layout, wealth of parks, and almost Mediterranean climate, is a most attractive city. Its peaceful suburbs sprawl down to almost Victorian-style seaside resorts and quiet beaches. And the state itself is one of vast contrasts: from those beach-side resorts to the isolation of the empty outback in the north of the state; from the craggy and isolated mountains of the Flinders Ranges to the Continental atmosphere of the vineyards of the Barossa Valley; and from the meandering waters of the Murray River to the offshore delights of Kangaroo Island, a popular holiday resort around which the waters teem with fish.

South Australia

Arrive in Adelaide by air from Melbourne or Sydney, as most visitors do, and you will warm to it immediately. The plane swoops in low over the soft, rolling Mount Lofty Ranges which form a pretty backdrop to Adelaide – as well as the site of its most pricey suburbs – before landing at an airport which, for the present at least, still has a distinctly small-town atmosphere. En route into the town centre, your taxi or airport bus will follow not a motorway, but peaceful suburban streets before crossing the ring of parkland which completely surrounds the city centre.

Adelaide is there not because it was ever a penal colony, but because of the dreams of a number of very far-sighted and determined men. The first of these was Captain Charles Sturt, who explored the Murrumbidgee and Murray Rivers and followed their route for 2560 kilometres through what is now South Australia to the sea. He in turn sent glowing reports back to London about his 'new fair discovery' of the central coastline of South Australia, and these reports fired the imagination of liberal reformer Edward Gibbon Wakefield, who at the time was serving a three-year jail sentence for abducting an heiress. Wakefield promptly set about planning a colony of free settlers in Australia, and upon his release formed the Colonisation Society whose aim was to found such a colony. Because of his record, Wakefield had great trouble in getting his ideas – which included the theory that if land was sold too cheaply in a new colony you would get settlers easily enough, but would attract no labour force – listened to. But eventually the politicians listened, and in 1834 the South Australia Foundation Act was passed and this duly laid down that land must be sold at a minimum of 12 shillings (about $A1) an acre. Captain John Hindmarsh was appointed as governor of the fledgling state and his friend and rival, Colonel William Light, was named as surveyor-general with powers to choose the site for, and plan, the state's capital.

Hindmarsh and a shipload of settlers and their livestock set off for Australia on board a battered old ship called the *Buffalo*, and the journey – commemorated in a vivid sound-and-light performance now shown in Adelaide – was a long and uncomfortable one. The *Buffalo* arrived in Port Lincoln on 17 December 1836, to join a number of pioneer ships which had arrived earlier, and later moved to Holdfast Bay. On 28 December, Governor Hindmarsh stood under an old gum tree (which can still be seen), and recited the Orders in Council which proclaimed South Australia to be a British province. The settlers spread themselves out along the

South Australia

coast, and on to Kangaroo Island. South Australia was born.

On paper, at least, it was a model colony. The governor's proclamation had stated that the aboriginal population had equal rights with Europeans, and a Protector of Aborigines was appointed. In fact the aboriginals had no money with which to 'buy' their own land, and indeed had no understanding of money. They were willing to labour on the settlers' farms in return for food, but saw no reason why that food should not be the 'white man's kangaroo', which they hunted, caught and killed. The white man's kangaroo didn't take a lot of hunting – for it was kept in fields and had a woolly white coat. The Protector of Aborigines did not have many problems in caring for the aboriginals, but he did get a lot of complaints from the settlers about the slaughter of their sheep.

The aboriginals, for their part, saw no reason why they should not continue to hunt on their traditional hunting grounds, and armed clashes eventually took place. A certain amount of lawlessness developed. But, in general, the settlement of South Australia was far more peaceful than the foundation of other early states.

Meanwhile, Colonel William Light had picked as the site for his capital the eastern side of Gulf St Vincent. In 1836 he had stood, so local legend has it, on what is now Montefiore Hill, in North Adelaide, overlooking the rather grubby river which Adelaide enlivens with the name 'the mighty Torrens,' and declared: 'The site of Adelaide shall be there.' The city was named after the wife of King William IV, and Light planned his 'vision' with care and foresight. He saw Adelaide as a central grid covering one square mile, encompassing the River Torrens, and with all the streets intersecting one another at right angles. Around this central grid would be a belt of green parkland, at least half-a-mile wide, which could not be built on. Although he did not know it, Light had designed the world's first 'green belt'.

Light had to work under considerable pressures – both pressure of time, as the population of the new colony grew rapidly, and pressure from officials and settlers who wanted him to change or modify his plans for the sake of expediency. His health was failing too, but he was an extremely determined man and, as any old soldier should do, he stuck firmly to his guns. 'I will let the future generations be the final judges,' he said, dismissively, to his critics. And although his city was far from complete by the time of his death in 1839, the concept at least was relatively safe.

I say 'relatively safe' because Light further planned that Adelaide should, in the fullness of time, expand outwards in an orderly fashion.

South Australia

In fact, the settlers built where they chose, and Adelaide sprawled towards, and then up, the Mount Lofty Ranges. But the green belt remained – and still remains – virtually inviolate, and I do not think that the colonel would be too displeased with the fulfilment of his schemes. He wanted future generations to judge, and their judgment (and one which I wholeheartedly share) is that, after the picturesquely sited Sydney and Perth, Adelaide is Australia's most attractive city. Colonel Light looks over it still: his statue, 'Light's Vision', stands on Montefiore Hill gazing over the city he created and his grave, in Light Square, is surmounted by a replica of his surveyor's theodolite.

Although its beginnings were so small, and historically insignificant, it is interesting to see how the circumstances of Adelaide's foundation have affected the city, and therefore the state of South Australia as a whole.

A century or so ago, the new colony was always looking a trifle anxiously over its shoulder at the 'convict colony' of New South Wales – indeed the site for the settlement was chosen partly because of its remoteness from New South Wales and the protection that such distance would afford. Today it is still somehow a place apart in Australia, with an atmosphere all its own. Its people are inordinately proud of the fact that their forefathers went there by choice – an attitude which does not always endear them to their neighbours. And Governor Hindmarsh's original declaration ruled that the settlers should conduct themselves 'with order and quietness, duly to respect the laws, by a course of sobriety and the practice of sound morality' – all habits which, at least until very recently, Adelaide's citizens followed with some dedication and which, in the process, earned Adelaide the unenviable reputation of being Australia's dullest city.

Today, it is almost pathetically eager to point out that it *is* moving with the times. The tourist can, if he is so minded, find a topless bar, and outside the town Maslin Beach was the first official nude beach in Australia. Friends in the city warned me over and over again of the inadvisability of venturing down Hindley Street, which they described as the red light area, alone at night. This ensured that I did take a lone midnight stroll down Hindley Street, and although it has more than its fair share of bars, clip joints, and groups of wandering youngsters, I have seen far livelier scenes in little English villages on a Saturday night. You could happily take the vicar for a walk down Hindley Street, and ensure that he was not even remotely shocked.

South Australia

One is perfectly safe, too – in Hindley Street or wandering across the wooded green belt at night. Muggings are unknown, and Adelaide does not even seem to have the occasional robust drunk that one might come across in other Australian cities. Law-abiding sobriety and morality are, at least on the surface, still a way of life in Adelaide.

The all-pervading atmosphere of a pre-war English provincial town is heightened at weekends, when the city 'closes down' at Saturday lunch-time and the people – more reserved than elsewhere in Australia – head for their homes, their families, the beach, or the wide open spaces of the Flinders Ranges. If it is ever to attract tourists who are not visiting friends and relatives, then Adelaide is going to have to do something about weekends, and either provide more entertainment possibilities or else draw the visitor's attention to exactly what is available.

At the moment, the city is best-known for its Adelaide Festival Centre, a spectacularly modern multi-purpose arts complex in Elder Park which is the setting of the famous biennial Adelaide Festival (held in March in even-numbered years) and attracts many famous international performers. Beside it, the damned River Torrens forms the narrow Lake Torrens. The Torrens, incidentally, lies at the heart of long-standing complaints about Adelaide's water supply. The earliest settlers used to complain that aboriginals performed their ablutions in the river, which at that time provided their fresh water supplies. Today the aboriginals have gone, and the water comes from other sources, but it is still to be avoided by visitors: Adelaide is the only city in Australia where the water is suspect.

The Festival Centre includes a main, 2000-seat concert hall and theatre and a 650-seat drama theatre, both with superb acoustics; an outdoor amphitheatre seating 1200 people; and a 350-seat experimental theatre called The Space. Not only the scenery but also the interior of the main concert hall can be changed at will by means of retractable roller blinds, and the hall contains the world's largest transportable organ which moves around on a cushion of air. There are hourly guided tours of the Festival Centre daily, except Sundays.

Adelaide is a very easy city in which to get your bearings and find your way around. The 688 hectares of parkland are pleasant places in which to stroll or relax, and these include the 16-hectare (40-acre) Botanic Gardens and Park, which are filled with native Australian vegetation; and the compact, adjoining zoo (open daily). Both are an easy stroll from almost anywhere in the city centre, but the zoo can also be reached by river launch from the Festival Centre.

South Australia

Wide King William Street is the main thoroughfare – leading from the banks of the Torrens to Victoria Square, which contains the grandiose Town Hall and GPO Building (the latter is the official centre of the city). A free 'Bee-line' bus links Victoria Square with the railway station in North Terrace, via King William Street. Shopping is for the most part in King William Street and in Rundle Street Mall, which runs off King William Street parallel with North Terrace. Rundle Street Mall is a very attractive, pedestrianised, shopping precinct lined with boutiques and cafés but also containing the city's major department stores (Myers, and David Jones, are probably the best).

The Old Parliament House, in North Terrace, contains the fascinating sound-and-light presentation of South Australia's earliest history mentioned earlier, and other buildings to see in the city include the Art Gallery of South Australia, in North Terrace (open daily, and Sunday afternoons), which contains a fine collection of paintings and other works of art from all over the world as well as some notable South-East Asian ceramics; the nearby South Australian Museum (open daily), which has probably the world's largest collection of aboriginal artefacts as well as an important Melanesian collection; and the historic home of Ayers House, also in North Terrace. Ayers House is an elegant bluestone building which was once the home of former South Australian premier Sir Henry Ayers. Today it is the headquarters of the South Australian National Trust, and contains an historical museum (there are tours on weekday afternoons, except Mondays), a good restaurant, and a bistro.

Eating out, it should be emphasised, is one of the unexpected pleasures of Adelaide: the restaurants in and around the city are of surprising variety, exceptionally high standard, and excellent value. Among the best, but not necessarily the most famous, is the Grapevine Restaurant in the Old Lion Hotel (Melbourne Street, North Adelaide); Decca's Place, also in Melbourne Street; the Oyster Bed, on the main northeast road; a Greek restaurant, the Ellinis, in Gouger Street; the Spanish-style Los Amigos, in Chesser Street; and the Swiss-style Schonenberg Restaurant. You can also eat well at the Buckingham Arms, in Walkerville, and some fascinating new restaurants are springing up in the hills and resorts around Adelaide to compete with older-established German restaurants owned and run by Adelaide's large German community. There are so many of these that it is hard to be selective, but try Maximilian's, a converted farmhouse in the hills at Verdun, 27 kilometres from the city centre; the boisterous Jolly Swagman, at Littlehampton; Vanessa's, a restaurant in an old church at Willunga; or the very German Mill Restaurant in Hahndorf, where you sit at a large communal table and eat roast suckling pig.

Hotel accommodation in the city is a trifle sparse, but the efficient – if quiet – Grosvenor Hotel, in North Terrace, can be recommended. Better, though, to stay with friends or relatives, or perhaps seek less formal, and much cheaper, accommodation away from the town centre in one of Adelaide's seaside resorts. These resorts have familiar names for Britons – names like Brighton, Henley, or Largs – but they are largely little more than seaside suburbs. One exception is Glenelg, which is linked with central Adelaide by the city's only tram service: it has the air of a resort about it, even if it is a faintly diffident, pre-war style resort. Also in the southern suburbs, there is a nice night-time panorama of the city to be seen from a promontory in the foothills of the Mount Lofty Ranges, known as Windy Point. The city fathers have, at various times, attempted to give Windy Point other, more prestigious names, so it may be hard to find on the map. But stop and ask a local for Windy Point, and you will get directions. The people of Adelaide may appear to differ from other Australians, but they share the national contempt for authority: Windy Point it is, and Windy Point it will remain.

A pleasant afternoon drive from Adelaide is around the Southern Vales, to the south of the city. This is farming and – increasingly – vineyard country, close to the sea. The vineyards are small and usually privately owned and operated – for dabbling in wine-growing is a popular pastime for South Australians, who are increasingly knowledgeable about the subject. Another popular pastime is to own or hire a caravan, or to camp out, on the beaches leading down to the Fleurieu Peninsula. Both beaches and countryside are slightly East Anglian in appearance and atmosphere. One passes Christies Beach, Port Noarlunga, and the nude Maslin Beach before turning inland to the charming little village of Willunga and the vineyards. Above Willunga stretch the Mount Lofty Ranges, with their pine forests, hiking trails, and conservation parks (there is a good one at Mount Magnificent, very close to Willunga). From Willunga, the road to the south heads down to Victor Harbour, which is a favourite seaside resort with South Australians, and the swimming and surfing beaches on the southern shore of the Fleurieu Peninsula. En route, at Mount Compass, the villagers – for reasons best known to themselves – stage an annual race between local cows

South Australia

for the Compass Cup, which at least serves to demonstrate that South Australia is not quite as straightlaced as it might appear to be on the surface. The inland road back to Adelaide twists and turns its way through the foothills again, or alternatively through the farmland around Clarendon.

Kangaroo Island, off the tip of the Fleurieu Peninsula 113 kilometres south of Adelaide, is the third largest island in Australia (after Tasmania and Melville), and has become a popular holiday destination because of its rich wildlife, its superb fishing, and its away-from-it-all atmosphere. It is a 35-minute flight from Adelaide, and there are also car ferry services to the island from Port Adelaide three times a week.

The island got its name from no less a person than the explorer Matthew Flinders, who took shelter from a storm there in 1802 and found that the kangaroos were so tame and inquisitive that he was able to replenish his ship's meat supply without any effort. Almost immediately after Flinders' visit, the island – which at 160 kilometres long and up to 55 kilometres wide has a surprising amount of room in which to hide – became the haunt of escaped convicts (who fled there and settled in 1806), smugglers and other undesirables; and later it served briefly as a whaling station.

Today it is visited mainly by outdoor enthusiasts: bush walkers, anglers (beach, rock, boat, river, jetty and spear fishing are all available, and there are charter cruises out to deeper waters for big game fishermen), explorers (the coastline is littered with wrecks) and nature lovers. The latter are in for a surprise, if they have not been to the island before. Despite their experience at the hands of Flinders and his successors, the various species of wildlife are still remarkably tame, and instead of them having to be protected from mankind it is now the other way round! The island's kangaroos, for example, are famous for their picnic hamper pilfering abilities. Other forms of fauna are plentiful, particularly fur seals and the diminutive fairy penguins; but one can also see all of Australia's most famous residents, including emus, koalas, possums, goanna lizards, and even the rare duck-billed platypus. There is plenty of accommodation on the island, ranging from hotels and motels to self-catering apartments, lodges and cabins. The rugged southwestern end of the island offers the best walking and hiking country.

If Kangaroo Island is a somewhat unexpected attraction to find in South Australia, then there are plenty more. In the far southeast of the state, 468 kilometres from Adelaide, the Mount Gambier pine

South Australia

forest is the largest in the country, and the region is noted for the beautiful volcanic crater of Blue Lake, a 170-metre deep lake which changes colour dramatically with the seasons. North of Adelaide lies a rather better-known playground, the peaks of the Flinders Ranges, which are a slice of the outback but come complete with colourful cliffs, granite peaks, razor-backed ridges and deep gorges.

The Flinders Ranges, rising to a height of 1160 metres, are also home to large numbers of native Australian birds and animals, and many Adelaide families like to drive out to the wilderness at weekends, or during their holidays, and camp. It is a wonderful area for exploring – complete with aboriginal paintings and rock carvings, and long-abandoned, half-forgotten mining towns. Wilpena Pound, in the heart of the Flinders Ranges, has modern motel accommodation and organised camping sites; while Arkaroola, 644 kilometres north of Adelaide, is a fauna sanctuary close to spectacular mountain and river scenery and of great interest to geologists (visitors can hunt for gemstones). Motel accommodation and camping and caravan parks can be found in Arkaroola Village.

Much closer to Adelaide itself is the charming countryside of the Barossa Valley, only 55 kilometres north of the capital and the home of 36 vineries which between them produce what I believe to be the best wines in Australia – and, in some cases, among the best wines in the world.

Only 30 kilometres long and eight kilometres wide, the valley was first settled in 1839 when German refugees fleeing from religious persecution in Silesia made their home in a little village which they called Bethany. The refugees laid out orchards and olive groves, and in their spare time they dabbled in making a potent pineapple wine. The latter was such a success that vines were planted and in 1850 one of the settlers, Johann Gramp, made the first sizeable bottling of Barossa wine – a hock. Other settlers followed his example, and in the space of 20 years the valley was transformed into an area founded on viniculture.

Since 1870, the Barossa Valley probably hasn't changed greatly. It was, and still is, an area with a distinctly German atmosphere about it. The three towns – Tanunda (the commercial centre), Nuriootpa and Angaston – are neat, tidy, and well laid-out, and are crowned by the tall spires of Lutheran churches. The bars tend to be beer gardens; the restaurants serve German food; and the bakeries have windows full of freshly baked German-style bread and fattening pastries and cakes.

South Australia

Perhaps the towns have spread a little over the years – along with their inhabitants' waistlines. Certainly the neat vineyards have crept higher up the hills which ring the valley, for the viniculturists have discovered that the higher vines produce different, sweeter wine. And the principal vineyards have built for themselves magnificent chateau-style headquarters which look as though they are relics of the fifteenth century but are usually more like circa 1960. Never mind, a vineyard is a vineyard, and the Barossa has something which most of Australia so patently lacks: a sense of tradition.

One can feel it when one ascends to Menglers Hill Viewpoint, from which one can see almost all of the semi-circular valley. South Australia's nineteenth-century German refugees divided themselves between the Adelaide suburb of Hahndorf and the Barossa Valley, and one suspects that, with hindsight at least, the 15 adventurous families who chose the Barossa Valley were the wisest. Things have not always been easy for them, of course. Because they have stuck to their own cultural identity (a form of German, Barossa Deutsch, is still spoken in the valley), they have sometimes been treated as outcasts: they faced, and in many cases suffered, internment during two world wars. Nevertheless, they have created a little bit of paradise.

Most of the wineries welcome visitors, and besides providing you with a guided tour they also provide liberal tastings of their product at no charge. Naturally, they hope to sell you a bottle or two – or a crate or two – of their wine, but despite that these free wine-tastings are still extraordinary to European eyes. If the great Champagne houses of France were to offer free tastings to all-comers, there would be a traffic jam right down to the Alps. In the tasting rooms of the Barossa Valley, on a summer's afternoon, you may find only a handful of people sipping appreciatively at their glasses – and those sippers will more often than not be serious shoppers for wine, rather than tourists in search of a free binge.

The wineries are, because of their stately headquarters, more than a little eye-catching in their agrarian surroundings. One, the turreted, castle-style headquarters of the Karlsburg winery, is irreverently referred to locally as 'Disneyland'. Others, like Seppeltsfield, where the Seppelt winery (one of the oldest, and the largest family-owned vineyard in Australia) is located, are more stately. Seppelt's Cabernet is, in my opinion, Australia's best wine. The Seppelt winery tours are particularly impressive, and are made all the more so when one considers that its founder, Joseph Seppelt, originally intended to grow tobacco in the area, not vines. There are self-contained holiday cabins to let on the estate.

There is some other accommodation in the area, but mostly the Barossa Valley is seen as a place to be visited on day trips from Adelaide. The valley, is, of course, at its best in the autumn, when the grapes are harvested, and every two years (in odd-numbered years, to avoid clashing with the Adelaide Festival), a week after Easter, the celebrations are extended into a boisterous four-day carnival known as the Vintage Festival.

In the valley, the Pheasant Restaurant is supposedly the best – but there are many to choose from, and most of them specialise in traditional German meats, sausages, cheesecake and pastries. I particularly like the German-run Die Weinstube Restaurant, just south of Marieoopa. For children, there is entertainment at Storybook Cottage, and they will enjoy the 'Whispering Wall' at the Barossa Reservoir.

And from a bit of Germany to a bit of typical Australiana. On the road back into Adelaide, it is worth stopping for a glass of cold beer at the Sandy Creek Hotel, a pub as Australian in its atmosphere and clientele as one could ever wish for. Local rumour has it that there is never any trouble in the Sandy Creek Hotel – for the landlady is a formidable woman with an extensive vocabulary and a strong right arm, and with a reputation for doing her own chucking out.

Another excellent excursion from Adelaide is a day, or a week, on the wide Murray River, which makes the last 650 kilometres of its 2600-kilometre journey to the sea through South Australia, before finally emptying itself into Lake Alexandrina, on the coast near Adelaide. From Goolwa, close to the point where a narrow strip of land almost (but not quite) separates the lake from the sea, the paddle-wheeler *Murray River Queen* makes five-day cruises up to Swan Reach and back, while another five-day cruise operates between Renmark and Morgan on the *Murray Explorer*. There are also houseboats – both of the static variety and stern-wheelers – for hire at the riverside towns of Renmark, Berri, Mannum and Murray Bridge.

The *Murray River Queen* cruise is a particularly restful and interesting one, although it could not be recommended for children (a houseboat, however, would be ideal for family holidays). The big stern-wheel paddle-steamer is a well-equipped and friendly boat, with nice cabins and huge public rooms, which makes its leisurely way up and down the wide, slow-moving river and makes overnight

South Australia

stops at various towns along the way. The countryside through which one passes is varied, if not exactly dramatic: orchards and vineyards, high limestone cliffs, and lush pastureland. Crew members point out all the features of interest, including the many varieties of birds and the local River Red Gum trees and the 'canoe trees' from the bark of which aboriginals used to make their canoes.

Northwest of Adelaide, at the head of the deep inlet of the Spencer Gulf, lies Port Augusta – a town 328 kilometres from the capital and situated, quite literally, at the crossroads of the southern half of the Australian continent. It is an important road and rail junction. Here the 'Indian Pacific' train from Adelaide to Perth starts its long journey across the empty wastelands of the Nullarbor Plain – passing over, en route, the world's longest stretch of straight railway track (478 kilometres). Here, too, the various roads from southeast Australia meet and converge and leave you with only two outbound roads from which to choose: north, to Alice Springs, or west, along the shores of the Great Australian Bight and on to Perth.

There is a brief alternative, in the shape of the peaceful wheatlands of the Eyre Peninsula, to the south – but even that road eventually links up with the one to Perth. And here one should perhaps repeat the warning that inter-state driving in Australia is not recommended, unless that is the specific purpose of your holiday. Distances can be vast, and roads can be rough. This particularly applies to the roads leading out of Port Augustus: it could take a week or more to drive west, to Perth and the northern route to Alice Springs is a heart-breaker (and, as one friend of mine found out to his cost, a car-breaker too).

There is a metalled road to the north as far as Woomera (where the weapons testing range is well known, but not a tourist attraction), but from then on the grandly named Stuart Highway becomes a dirt road. Such roads are immensely dangerous, especially when they are crossing some of Australia's harsher desert land. Between November and March the heat can be so intense that electric light bulbs will explode. At other times, rain can make the road impassable for days at a time. People who do intend to undertake such trips should seek advice from the Royal Automobile Association of South Australia before they set out, and should carry plenty of drinking water, food and petrol. If you intend to leave the major roads, a four-wheel drive vehicle is essential – but many side roads in the South Australian outback are closed anyway to people who do not have a Ministry of Defence permit. Of course, motorists

South Australia

do drive up to Alice Springs – but most find the trip totally exhausting for both the car and its occupants, and choose to make the return half of the journey by train.

A friend, who did the trip as his holiday, reports being in a state of mental and physical exhaustion by the time he reached Coober Pedy, 960 kilometres from Adelaide in the far northwest of the state – and he still had several days' driving ahead of him. He did eventually make it to Alice – but the car didn't.

Coober Pedy is an extraordinary frontier town whose name is an aboriginal phrase meaning 'man who lives in a hole'. Summer temperatures are so high (sometimes reaching 50°C) that many of the town's residents do indeed live in holes – for they have built their often surprisingly comfortable homes underground. Even the town's church is underground. The people are there because Coober Pedy sits on top of – or perhaps one should say in buried within – the world's largest-known opal fields. Visitors can buy a permit and fossick for opals and other gems if they wish – but it is hard work. One can also fossick for opals at Andamooka, 622 kilometres north of Adelaide, but again a mining permit is necessary. There is some tourist accommodation in both towns (above ground in Coober Pedy, you may be glad to learn), but it is extremely limited.

It is hard to realise that Coober Pedy is more or less at the centre of South Australia. One has to fly over the state to realise the extent of it – and much of it is simply desert. The only other road – if one can call it that – is the Birdsville Track, a difficult cross-country route leading from the one-time camel train centre of Marree up into Queensland (see also Chapter 10), for which one would need a four-wheel drive vehicle, camping equipment, and plenty of time. But South Australia does contain one other noteworthy curiosity: the world's sixteenth largest lake.

This is Lake Eyre, to the north of Marree. And if you have never heard of it, that is not too surprising because it has water in it only after prolonged rain, which happens in these parts on average only once in every 50 years. For most of the time, Lake Eyre is nothing but a huge, glistening white bed of salt. Oddly enough, one of the streams which runs into Lake Eyre, Cooper's Creek, is filled with fish which are very easy to catch in the water-holes into which the river subsides.

Much of this area is still largely unexplored on foot. It was only recently that archaeologists discovered, in the dried-up bed of Lake Callabonna, the fossilised remains of the diprotodon, or giant

South Australia

wombat, the largest-known marsupial, which died out 16,000 years ago. The diprotodon is thought to have perished when he became stuck in the fast-drying mud, and who knows what other secrets this vast area may be keeping? But the holidaymaker should not go looking for these secrets except as part of a properly organised and properly equipped expedition – unless that is, he is prepared to risk becoming an archaeological discovery himself in another 16,000 years' time.

9 Tasmania

Whether by accident or design, Australians can be remarkably ignorant about the country's smallest state – the island of Tasmania, 240 kilometres south of Melbourne across the windswept waters of the Bass Strait. Visitors to the island have been known to bring along their passports with them, attempt to change currency – and one even expressed a wish to go back home to Melbourne by bus. The better-informed speak slightingly of 'cutting the rope' and letting Tasmania drift away into the southern oceans.

The Tasmanians are not amused. They call themselves Tasmanians, rather than Australians, and refer to the Australian mainland as 'that island to the north'. History and geography have both decreed that Tasmania should be something of a poor relation in the Australian scheme of things, but the Tasmanians are tired of being underrated and patronised. One islander, his tongue perhaps loosened by a few glasses of beer, turned to me with real anger in his voice and declared: 'I say "bugger the mainlanders". They think they have got everything over there. But we know that we have got it here, on the island.'

He had a point, for Tasmania is a remarkably pleasant island enjoying a tourism boom. But its geographical and historical disadvantages are considerable. Because Australia is so immense, maps seem to suggest that Tasmania is a very small island, and that it is just off the coast of the mainland. In fact, Tasmania is roughly the same size as Scotland; and New Guinea is closer to Australia's northern coast than Tasmania is to its southern coast.

Today, several flights a day link Melbourne with Hobart and Launceston, and a car ferry plies to and fro across the Bass Strait between Melbourne and Devonport – ties which connect the island firmly with Australia. Mainland Australians are beginning to see what they call 'Tassy' (pronounced 'Tazzy') as a holiday destination very different from anything they have at home: whether the attraction is Tasmania's hill country, its liberal licensing hours, or its legalised gambling. But that has not always been the case, for the earliest settlers saw Tasmania as an ugly and inhospitable island best suited as a dumping ground for the people who weren't wanted on the mainland – and to be unwanted in an Australian convict settlement you had to be pretty bad. Tasmania had a harsh history as a penal colony, and it is estimated that even today one in six of the island's 425,000 residents is descended from a convict – perhaps from a convict of the worst kind! This, of course, is a cause of considerable satisfaction among mainland Australians, who get tired of being reminded about their own criminal antecedents, and their teasing attitude towards the islanders on occasions is doubtless a major cause of any tension that there may be.

There are three major aspects to Tasmania: its horrific history; its pleasant cities, of which Hobart and Launceston are the two main ones; and its glorious coastline and countryside which, for once, has probably benefited from the attempts of man to improve upon the landscape (the early settlers found the wilderness unsettling, and worked hard to produce successfully large areas of pastoral, and even sylvan, landscape). Together these factors combine to produce the visitor's reaction to the island. Some find its unhappy past is something which cannot be put out of your mind, and that places like the convict settlement at Port Arthur, which must have experienced so much unhappiness and despair, have a melancholy and even haunted air about them which can seep into your soul and prevent you ever really relaxing and enjoying yourself. Others find the nightlife of the cities, and particularly the casinos, invigorating. And others again, particularly hikers and campers, find the variety of coastal and inland scenery – ranging from rugged mountains and moorland to deserted beaches, and from impenetrable bush to tidy, blossom-filled apple orchards – a fascinating contrast to the Australian mainland.

Tasmania is roughly triangular in shape, 296 kilometres deep and ranging from 315 kilometres wide in the north of the island to only about 70 kilometres wide in the south. It was discovered by Europeans in 1642, when Anthony Van Diemen, governor of the Dutch settlements in the East Indies, sent Abel Janszoon Tasman out on a voyage of discovery around the shores of the vast Australian continent which they knew existed to the south but which no-one had yet really explored. Tasman sighted the mountainous west coast

12 Christmas celebrations Australian-style: on the beach near Melbourne.

13 City tram in Collins Street, Melbourne – Victoria's state capital.

14 The two faces of Australia: a freckle-faced youngster and a sulphur-crested cockatoo at Melbourne Zoo.

15 The Festival Centre in Adelaide, capital of South Australia.

16 The pleasure paddle steamer *Murray River Queen* on the Murray River in South Australia.

17 Vineyards in the Barossa Valley, South Australia.

18 Small is dangerous: the Tasmanian devil is Australia's fiercest mammal.

19 Constitution Docks, Hobart, Tasmania: a centre for deep-sea sailors.

20 Yachts competing in the annual Sydney-to-Hobart Race tied up at Constitution Docks, Hobart, Tasmania.

21 Richmond Bridge, Tasmania: a relic of the island's convict days.

22 One of nature's mysteries: the tesselated pavement at Eaglehawk Neck, Tasmania.

23 Ruins of the church at the once-infamous penal colony of Port Arthur, Tasmania.

24 On the beach at Heron Island, Great Barrier Reef, Queensland.

of the island on 24 November, and sailed around the southern tip of the island to what is now called Storm Bay, at the mouth of the Derwent River where Hobart now stands. The bay got its name because Tasman's ship could not anchor in the rough weather, and was eventually swept back out to sea. Eventually, round the east coast, the ship's carpenter was despatched to swim ashore and plant the Dutch flag, and Tasman named his discovery Van Diemen's Land, in honour of the governor who had sent him.

Tasman sailed on, eventually to discover New Zealand, and it was not for another 130 years that another European visitor was to arrive there. This was a Frenchman, in 1772, and he was rapidly followed by a member of Captain Cook's expedition and then, in 1777, by Captain Cook himself, who landed at Adventure Bay. In 1798 Bass and Flinders sailed right round Tasmania, proving it to be an island, and in 1802 it was formally claimed for England on orders from Sydney because of fears of French colonisation. The first settlement took place at Risdon, near Hobart, on 11 September 1803; the north of the island was settled in 1804; and within a very short time both northern and southern inhabitants decided to move their settlements by just a few kilometres: the northerners to Launceston, and the southerners to present-day Hobart.

For nearly half a century, however, the new colony was used by both Britain and Sydney as a dumping ground for the very worst of their convicts, with Sydney shipping across the Bass Strait – known to the convicts as 'the passage between heaven and hell' – the transported criminals whom even they had been unable to tame. There was an early, and very harsh, convict settlement on the exposed west coast, but the most famous was at Port Arthur, in the southeast corner of the island, which a couple of very narrow and easily guarded necks of land turn into a natural prison. Conditions at Port Arthur were appalling, and the discipline cruel. A number of prisoners did escape, to live as outlaws in the bush. These escapers terrorised the free settlers, and fought with the aboriginals – and the aboriginals were in turn hired by the authorities to try to track down the escapers.

Besides being inundated with white criminals, the settlers in Tasmania were unfortunate in their dealings with the aboriginals. The first landings on the island suggested that there were human inhabitants there, but they were not seen and a rumour arose that Tasmania was the home of a race of giants. Then, in 1772, when the French made a landing, one aboriginal was shot.

Tasmania

So it was in an atmosphere of mutual racial suspicion that the first white settlement at Risdon took place. And in 1804 frightened settlers, who saw a group of about 300 aboriginals racing through the bush behind a flock of kangaroos, feared that they were about to be attacked and called in the military. Troops fired a volley, killing several aboriginals, and a blood feud had begun. White settlers were murdered, aboriginals were killed in retaliation (one group were herded over a clifftop by shepherds), and between 1825 and 1830 the feud reached the proportions of a mini-war. Eventually the tough disciplinarian governor, Sir George Arthur, decided that drastic measures were needed, and in October 1830 he launched the 'Black Line' – a sweep by 5000 troops and settlers right across the eastern half of the island with the intention of herding the aboriginals onto the Forestier Peninsula. Aboriginal bush-craft proved superior to that of their pursuers, and the sweep was a resounding failure: between them, the 5000 huntsmen captured only one man and a boy.

In fact, aboriginal numbers were dwindling dramatically anyway. Where the sweep had failed, an evangelist called George Robinson and some aboriginal friends were more successful: they went into the bush and persuaded many aboriginals to leave for Flinders Island, in the Bass Strait. The few that remained moved as a group to Oyster Cove in 1847, but they seemed to have lost the will to live and the last full-blooded Tasmanian aboriginal, Truganini, died in Hobart in 1876. Obviously, in the circumstances, little scientific study has been made of these original inhabitants of Tasmania, but in 1802 a French naturalist showed that they were of a different race to the mainland aboriginals.

Perhaps it is surprising, in all the circumstances, that Tasmania survived as a colony. But it did. As Van Diemen's Land, it achieved independence from New South Wales in 1825 and became a separate colony. Its prospects of attracting free settlers improved dramatically in 1853, when the transportation of convicts ceased, and because the name 'Van Diemen's Land' sounded too much like 'Van Demon's Land', and had become associated all over Australia with crime and brutality, the settlers decided in 1856 to rename the island Tasmania, after its original discoverer. Telegraph links were established with Victoria, railway lines began to sprout around the island (the line from Hobart to Launceston was opened in 1876), and in 1877 the infamous Port Arthur penal settlement was finally closed down. In 1901, Tasmania duly joined the federation of the Commonwealth of Australia as a fully-fledged state.

Tasmania

Hobart, its capital, is one of the world's most ideally situated cities, nestling between the 1270-metres high Mount Wellington and the broad estuary of the River Derwent. Although it is about 20 kilometres upstream from the mouth of the river, it has a very fine deep-water harbour, and almost every one of the city's houses, which sprawl along both sides of the river, has a view of both water and mountains. It has not yet got too big: take a main road out of the city in any direction except north, and in 10 minutes you will be in the bush. And it claims Australia's most equable climate: with less rain than any other state capital (one supposes that this claim relates to volume rather than frequency), the second highest number of hours of sunshine, and the most daylight. The latter points are presumably connected, and anyway the sunshine record is also claimed by almost every other state capital. It might be safer to describe the weather as being similar to that of southern Britain or northern France.

The local tourist office insists that the natives are friendly. Perhaps they are, but they are also insular – and if that seems a silly thing to say about an island people, then it should be taken in the context of the outgoing, and even extrovert, character of the Australian people as a whole. I found the Tasmanians quiet and almost reserved – in fact, rather British. Underneath the reserve, however, they have an extraordinary strength of character which, though one hesitates to mention it, may not be entirely unconnected with their ancestry. Famous Tasmanians have included Errol Flynn and Merle Oberon, and the island also lays claim to Second World War hero Lord Montgomery, although in reality he only went to school there.

The other thing that one notices about Tasmanians is that they appear to be extraordinarily prosperous. The harbour is studded with yachts, but then Hobart is sailing-mad anyway. It is, of course, the finishing point for the annual Sydney-to-Hobart yacht race, and this is an event which gives Hobart its biggest annual opportunity to let its hair down. The ocean-going racing yachts, from all over the world, leave Sydney on 26 December (Boxing Day) every year and, although the record for the 1000-kilometre trip is now less than 36 hours, most arrive in Hobart either just before or on New Year's Eve. The yachts are crammed into every available inch of space around the town's Constitution Dock, and on shore the world's best, and most exclusive, New Year's Eve street party is staged.

Besides yachts, the Tasmanians seem to have money to spare for gambling, too. In 1973 Australia's first casino, the Wrest Point Casino, was opened in Hobart, and although other cities and other

Tasmania

states are now jumping on the bandwagon, the Wrest Point remains crammed with gamblers and onlookers alike, night after night, all year round. Even accepting that many of these people are tourists from overseas and from other parts of Australia, there seem to be an awful lot of local regulars.

Most, no doubt, are simply having their weekly night out – tempted to the Wrest Point Casino not only by the gambling opportunities, but what are arguably the best meals in Hobart and what are certainly the best cabaret shows that I have seen anywhere in Australia, featuring, most weeks, British TV and stage stars and other acts which would not be out of place in London's West End.

The Wrest Point Casino building, which is a circular tower block, dominates the Hobart skyline. Inside, the entertainment, gaming, and dining facilities are superb, and the staff are slick, but – as is often the case with circular hotel buildings – the bedrooms seem cramped. One hopes that this will be at least partly rectified with the completion of a hefty addition to the hotel, including a conference centre, on adjoining land which has been reclaimed from the sea.

But the casino, for all its architectural prominence, could not claim to be Hobart's principal building. That honour must go to the mighty Tasman Bridge, which soars across the Derwent to link Hobart, the eastern suburbs, and the airport. There is a spectacular view of the bridge to be had from Rosny Hill – and if the bridge looks a little cock-eyed to you, then you are right. It lost a span in 1972 when it was rammed by an oil tanker, but the Tasmanians mysteriously managed to complete three years of repairs without snarling up Hobart's traffic altogether. On the eastern shore, the Eastlands shopping complex – another claimant to the title of 'southern hemisphere's largest' – offers the best shopping in Hobart.

Besides such modern edifices, Hobart retains plenty of old buildings. In Battery Point, just outside the present town centre, Hobart's first residential area has been retained almost intact, and includes not only the large mansions of the early nineteenth-century merchants but a cluster of tiny cottages around Arthur Circus, at the heart of Battery Point, which once belonged to wharf labourers. Visitors can walk around the narrow streets of Battery Point at will, but there are also informative guided tours.

Other city highlights include the Tasmanian Maritime Museum, in Argyle Street, which has seafaring and whaling exhibits but is particularly interesting for its attempt to depict the lifestyle of the island's aboriginals (open daily); and the Allport Library and

Museum of Fine Arts, in Murray Street, which contains the eighteenth-century furniture, books, glass, silver and other possessions of the pioneering Allport family (open weekdays). There is also a folk museum in the fine colonial home at 103 Hampden Road, Sandy Bay (open daily, and weekend afternoons).

The street market held in Salamanca Place every Saturday morning in summer, complete with strolling musicians and street theatre in addition to the usual collection of market stalls, is one of the city's few traditions. Popular excursions in the vicinity of the city are up to the top of Mount Wellington, from which on a clear day it is possible to see a distance of 110 kilometres, and out to the historic colonial village of Richmond, off the road to Port Arthur. Richmond contains Australia's oldest bridge, built in 1823 and still in use; and Australia's oldest Catholic church, St John's, which was built in 1836.

Southeast of Hobart, the Tasman Peninsula is not only the most historic corner of the island but also one of the most beautiful. The road from Hobart bypasses Richmond, crosses a causeway at the head of Frederick Henry Bay, then plunges into a pastoral landscape of farms and woodland in which eucalyptus trees are mixed in with oak and ash – both introduced into Tasmania by homesick settlers. Compared with most of Australia, the island is very well wooded: it covers only 1 per cent of the nation's land area, yet contains 25 per cent of Australia's rain forests and 17 per cent of its high-quality eucalyptus forests.

A number of rather extraordinary tourist attractions have sprung up along the road to Port Arthur, but there could be none more extraordinary than the Copping Colonial Convict Exhibition, at Copping, about 40 kilometres east of Hobart. It consists of a huge, barn-like building filled with the biggest collection of bric-à-brac, much of it rusty, and gathering dust, that I have ever seen. Three life-sized working models of a pioneer blacksmith's shop, a washer-woman, and a bushmen's sharpening wheel perhaps entitle the collection to call itself a museum, but doubtless a thousand other items in the barn are articles of genuine historical interest and worthy of a museum place. What makes such items hard to spot is the fact that they are jumbled together with thousands of other items which are nothing more than honest-to-goodness junk – ranging from dusty seashells to a vast collection of well-chewed but not particularly ancient briar pipes.

The collection was built up by a somewhat eccentric local handyman called Jack Smith who also chose to decorate his garden,

Tasmania

and the adjoining lake, with a garish display of hand-made monsters and mermaids. He would never throw anything away, and people from all over the Tasman Peninsula used to bring him any old items which they dug up on farms, found in hedgerows, or turned out of attics – ranging from genuine convict artefacts to auntie's last set of false teeth. Jack Smith eventually sold out to a couple of Tasmanian entrepreneurs, for a very large sum of money, and that the entrepreneurs also knew what they were doing is suggested by the fact that, at the rate visitors are flocking to see the collection at present, they will have got their money back within five years. They plan extensions and renovations. Meanwhile, the barnful of valuable antiques and obviously not-quite-worthless rubbish remains what it has always been: a dusty, disorganised treasure house which, if it has done nothing else, has proved the truth of the old adage that where there's muck there's money.

At Dunalley the road crosses a narrow neck of land, where the Tasman Monument stands, in memory to Tasman's landing there, on the Forestier Peninsula. Then, after about 15 kilometres, an even narrower neck of land is reached: Eaglehawk Neck.

On the hill above Eaglehawk Neck there is a good viewpoint across the isthmus and, as an added attraction, the beach below comprises a geological curiosity known as the Tessellated Pavement. There the flat rocks look just like a man-made pavement of equal-sized, rectangular stones with mortar between them. But it was nature, not man, who put the pavement there.

Eaglehawk Neck, only a few metres across, virtually separates the Tasman Peninsula from the rest of Tasmania, and in the days when Port Arthur was a penal colony this made the peninsula very easy to guard. A line of fierce dogs was chained across Eaglehawk Neck and that alone, coupled with the convicts' fear of water, was enough to keep the prisoners where the government thought they belonged: there were very few escapes.

At Eaglehawk Neck, a brief diversion off the main road brings you to three other natural curiosities – and a man-made one. The man-made one is the tiny village of Doo Town, just beyond Eaglehawk Neck, where every house has to have a name and each one of those names has to include the word 'Doo'. Doo Little and Love Me Doo are a couple of the names which residents have chosen for their houses, but at present the village population does not seem to be expanding very quickly. I wonder why?

Tasmania

The Blowhole, Tasman's Arch and the Devil's Kitchen follow in rapid succession. The Blowhole is at its best in heavy seas, when jets of water erupt from it like lava from a volcano. Tasman's Arch is a spectacular natural rock bridge, whittled away over the centuries by the waves. But even the arch is not as spectacular as the Devil's Kitchen, where visitors stand on a clifftop and look straight down into a cauldron of churning surf hemmed in on three sides by sheer rock walls: it is dramatic even on a calm day, and is not recommended for sufferers from vertigo.

A few kilometres farther on, at Taranna, the Tasmanian Devil Park (open daily) is a fascinating little wildlife park devoted to the fauna of the island, but featuring the ferocious little Tasmanian devil (see also Chapter 3). Although it is only the size of a small terrier, and eats carrion rather than hunting for its prey, a cornered Tasmanian devil is the most savage mammal to be found in Australia. They will cheerfully attack a man, and even hand-reared ones cannot be tamed. Naturalist John Hamilton, the park's owner, is a fund of information about Tasmanian wildlife, on which he is an ackowledged expert, and he is very approachable.

Another very approachable man along the road to Port Arthur (there are so many attractions along this route that one wonders at tourists ever reaching their destination) is the former journalist who owns and runs the Bush Mill, a working reproduction of a nineteenth-century logging camp complete with wooden railed tramway and convict sawpit. The mill (open daily) includes an excellent audio-visual presentation of what life used to be like in the original Tasmanian logging camps, and there is a very good coffee shop. The Bush Mill is one of the best living museum complexes that I have seen. In fact, it could become too successful. When the mill found out how to split roof shingles – the wooden house tiles used on older houses all over the island, and now popular on new properties too – it discovered an industry with a large, ready-made market. Roof shingles now sell like hot cakes, and the mill appears to make rather more money from that than it does from the tourists.

Almost nextdoor to the Bush Mill, two kilometres north of Port Arthur, is the Tudor-style Fox and Hounds public house, which is trying very hard to be an English-style pub. It has not quite got the ambience right yet, but it does serve delicious pub lunches.

Perhaps all these distractions on the road to Port Arthur serve a purpose, because it is best to arrive at this sad spot in the late afternoon, after the crowds have departed. Although it served as a

Tasmania

penal colony for only 47 years, and the 12,500 prisoners who were sent there constructed a model town, Port Arthur was harshly run – and must have been the scene of a great deal of human suffering, and perhaps even greater despair, on the part of people who knew that they would never see their homes again. It is not idle romanticism to say that you can still feel the aura of despair there to this day.

This, I am sure, is enhanced by the fact that many of the buildings are ruins. The settlement was originally constructed for 'worst offender' prisoners because of the ease with which the peninsula could be guarded and because of the proximity of work for the constructional and other labour gangs (many convicts had to work in logging camps, standing in a pit and sawing through the huge logs above). Soon after it was abandoned in 1877, Port Arthur was burnt out by a bush fire, and it has since suffered another. These fires destroyed many of the old buildings, and the weather has done the rest. Several of those which do remain, like the penitentiary, the hospital, and the guardhouse, stand empty and roofless, their windows staring blindly into the distance, as ravaged as the bodies of the prisoners they once housed. Even the church, which still stands at the entrance to the site, is unconsecrated – because, so it is said, a murder took place there.

The commandant's residence (now a private house) and the asylum were the only buildings to escape the fires. Today the asylum houses a scale model of Port Arthur in the 1870s, an audio-visual theatre, and an excellent little museum which bears adequate witness to the hardship and cruelties endured by the prisoners. Further evidence, if it were needed, is to be found on the Isle of the Dead at the entrance to Port Arthur Bay. There are hourly launch trips out to the island – a grisly spot which is the last resting place of 1769 convicts (buried in mass graves) and 150 free settlers, soldiers, seamen, and their wives and children who died between 1833 and 1877. The convicts' graves are unmarked, but massive headstones erected over many of the 'free' graves carry inscriptions engraved by convicts and telling harrowing stories of harsh life.

For a spot of light relief, after all this sadness, there are some nice strolls around the outskirts of the settlement (try following the fishermen's path, to the left of the jetty), and a pottery run by two interesting women. Accommodation in the area is hard to find, however, and the Port Arthur campsite is not particularly pleasant.

South of Hobart, there is more attractive countryside along the shores of the D'Entrecasteaux Channel which separates the main-

Tasmania

land from the charming and historic Bruny Island – the site of Captain Cook's landing. Bruny Island, with its superb beaches, is almost two islands – but a narrow isthmus, almost 10 kilometres long, strings the two halves together. The sand dunes on this isthmus are the home of fairy penguins from August until April, and they are a fascinating sight as they return from the sea each evening at dusk and march up the beaches with food for their young.

The mainland beaches are good too, safe and well protected. They are popular with holidaymaking Tasmanian families, and good accommodation can be found at Cygnet (a wine-growing centre) or Dover. Behind such mini-resorts lie the Hartz Mountains, a national park area, unexplored, and indeed frequently inaccessible, bush. And the Hartz themselves are only a foretaste of Tasmania's wild southwest: an area of mountains, lakes, caves and waterfalls.

Mountain areas of Tasmania – and what has been described as 'the world's most mountainous island' has plenty of these – are much visited and much enjoyed by walkers, climbers, anglers (the island's trout fishing is superb), and campers. But it is important to stress that the fell land and the bush are two very different things. Tracks leading into the bush in the southwest do exist, but they should be attempted only by the hardiest and best-equipped of walkers, and then only after seeking local advice (preferably from the police). In the island generally, guided walks are advisable. Tasmania's bush is so dense that in places you have to walk on tree trunks which have been bent horizontal by the elements (the so-called Horizontal Forest); in other parts you have to cut a path for yourself; and in other parts a walker could be hopelessly lost in the lush undergrowth only moments after leaving a marked trail. It is little wonder that naturalists are still not sure exactly what creatures might be hiding in this inhospitable countryside.

Either Hobart or its northern rival, Launceston, makes a good base for touring the rest of the island. The direct road between them, the Midland Highway, passes through the very attractive Midlands region, and there are pleasant stops to be made at Kempton, Oatlands, Tunbridge, Ross (just off the Midland Highway) and Campbell Town. All are historic villages with their roots in Tasmania's earliest history, and were settled in the early part of the nineteenth century.

Best-known is the very attractive village of Ross, with its fine early colonial buildings and its beautiful stone bridge; the bridge was opened in 1836, and is one of Australia's finest historical monu-

Tasmania

ments. All of the later major buildings in the town were built of stone matching that of the bridge, which has given Ross an entity rarely to be found anywhere in Australia. The Scotch Thistle Inn, first licensed in 1830 as a coaching inn, has been restored as a fully licensed restaurant. The Beaufront Deer Park, eight kilometres from Ross, is a natural bush sanctuary stocked with deer and local fauna.

Kempton, closest of the Midland towns to Hobart, also has a good collection of original cottages and grand colonial houses, many of them still owned by relatives of the people who built them. The village bakery, McKay's, is famous all over the island. Oatlands, attractively situated on the shores of Lake Dulverton, a one-time quarry which now serves as a wildlife sanctuary, houses the largest collection of Georgian architectural styles to be found anywhere in Australia. The Callington Flour Windmill (1837) and the old Supreme Court House (1835) are two fine examples.

Tunbridge, 15 kilometres south of Ross and bypassed by the main road, has had to fight hard to keep its place on the tourist map, but it has succeeded due to the energetic creation of 'traditional' events (like an annual village fair in March which includes the Australian penny-farthing bicycle riding championships) and a remarkable musical museum called the Old Time Music Parlour. Tunbridge gets its name from Tunbridge Wells, in England, which was the home of Thomas Fleming, an immigrant who arrived in Tasmania in 1827 and hand-built the Tunbridge Wells Inn. The inn soon became an overnight stop for stage coaches travelling between Hobart and Launceston, but it eventually lost patronage to a newer hotel, changed its name and its purpose several times, and suffered a certain amount of disrepair. Now the inn has gone back to its original name, and has been most handsomely restored – even if it does still look like something out of the Wild West rather than rural Kent. At the opposite end of the town there is refreshment to be found at the Penny Farthing Tea Rooms – a popular training ground for those annual championships.

Farther north, Campbell Town is a former garrison town lacking the ambience of its neighbours but making up for that by its hotel and restaurant facilities as well as the many sporting opportunities in the immediate district.

Launceston is an attractive city, studded with gardens and parks which are shaded not only by Australian trees but by English oaks and elms, which seem to have taken quite happily to growing 12,000 miles away from their natural habitat. The city stands at the head of the Tamar estuary, but it is another local river, the South Esk, which provides Launceston's most famous sight: the rocky Cataract Gorge. The gorge is crossed by footbridge or chairlift, is particularly spectacular after heavy rain in the central highlands, and is also popular at night (there are restaurant facilities).

The 12-hectare City Park contains a colourfully stocked conservatory and a miniature zoo, while at Launceston Wildlife Sanctuary and Rhododendron Gardens, south of the city, there are more flora and fauna to be seen.

Launceston retains a number of very fine colonial-style buildings, which one can see just dotted around the town. The two best-known are the convict-built Franklin House, six kilometres from the city centre, which dates from 1838 and after seeing service as a school has been restored with period furniture and fittings (open daily); and Entally House, at Hadspen, 13 kilometres south of Launceston, which was built in 1820 and contains excellent antiques. But the town's major attraction is Penny Royal World, in Paterson Street – a fascinating collection of buildings constructed in early nineteenth-century style and including working water and windmills, a farmhouse, and craft shops – like the blacksmith's shop – which date from that period. Because of its suitability for families, Penny Royal World (open daily) is Tasmania's most popular tourist spot. Its restaurant facilities are very good.

The city has plenty of accommodation – with the new Launceston Country Club Casino and the contrastingly old and historic Colonial Motor Inn being probably the best – and a big choice of restaurants catering both for families and quiet candlelit dinners. It is also an excellent touring centre for the Tamar Valley or the north coast.

Tasmania's other principal towns – none of them with more than 20,000 inhabitants – are the Bass Strait ferry terminal and port of Devonport; the port of Burnie, farther west along the north coast; the coastal resort of Ulverston, midway between the two ports and a starting point for trips into the mountainous hinterland; New Norfolk, on the river Derwent north of Hobart; and Queenstown, on the mountainous west coast.

Motorists touring Tasmania, who will presumably wish to make at least one crossing of the island on the Midland Highway, are faced with a difficult choice when it comes to their other north-south route. Major roads out of Hobart head out both east and west, deep into the countryside, before eventually crossing the north of the island to meet up at Launceston.

Tasmania

The western route, which is the most popular, passes through New Norfolk. This is an historic town, containing both the oldest existing church in Tasmania – St Matthew's, in which the first service was held in 1825 – and what is claimed to be the Commonwealth's 'oldest continuous licensed hotel' (the Bush Inn, licensed in 1825). The road then follows the Derwent Valley up through the fruit and hop-growing 'basket' of Tasmania – with the Mount Field National Park, the vast Pedder-Gordon hydro-electric complexes, and huge areas of empty, unexplored bushland, away to the left. There is a very worthwhile detour up to Strathgordon and the Pedder and Gordon lakes, and the three-hour boat trip on the man-made Lake Gordon can be a spectacular one in the early morning sunshine (catch the 9 a.m. sailing).

Climbing out of the Derwent Valley the road reaches Derwent Bridge, which stands between Lake St Clair and Lake King William, in the Cradle Mountain and Lake St Clair National Park. This is wonderful camping country, and the site overlooking Lake St Clair is a spectacular and well-equipped one – but be prepared to make your own evening amusements.

There is a good view of Queenstown from Gormanston, just before the road drops down into this old but somewhat remote town. Queenstown's greatest asset is perhaps its assorted friendly pubs – good pubs are remarkably hard to find in Tasmania.

The road from Queenstown eventually meets the north coast just west of Burnie, and travellers with time to spare might find it worthwhile to take the west-bound road at least as far as Boat Harbour, a beach-side hamlet which overlooks a small white sandy cove and is well off the tourist track (despite which, the authorities have chosen to erect a modern and very out-of-place brick-built public convenience). There are a couple of motels, and a beachfront restaurant which may not look up to much but is run by two very pleasant girls and serves delicious, genuinely fresh, crayfish. From Boat Harbour, one can drive on to Stanley, at the northwest tip of the island, but it is rather disappointing.

The road from Hobart to Launceston up the eastern side of the island follows the coast for much of the way, and is pretty, if less interesting, than its rival route. Between Swansea and Bicheno, beach lovers should divert on to the minor road leading to Coles Bay, then take the track down to the Friendly Beaches –as beautiful and unspoilt a stretch of sand as one could find anywhere in Tasmania. How the Friendly Beaches got their name is a bit of a mystery – you

Tasmania

are highly unlikely to find anyone else there with whom to be friendly!

Bicheno is not a very exciting spot, but the evocatively named Chain of Lagoons is lovely, and the Elephant Pass, on the climb inland to St Mary's, is a famous viewpoint. To get the best of the scenery, one could leave the coast road at St Mary's, drive inland through Fingal and Evoca, in the shadow of the 1573-metre Ben Lomond (Tasmania's skiing centre), and meet up with the Midland Highway at Conara Junction. Just north of Conara Junction, however, one could turn off to the right and take the quieter, more scenic, and parallel route to Launceston through Nile and Evandale.

The point about driving around Tasmania, or indeed getting around the island by any other means, is that there is a very great deal to see and do, but that you are often going to hunt down side roads, or badly signposted tracks, to find them. But not only must care be taken on such excursions (if you get stuck down some of the remoter tracks, you might be there for ever), it must also be remembered that Australia's – and particularly Tasmania's – tourist infrastructure is in its infancy.

I have already mentioned the shortage of pubs, but that is not a very serious omission (or perhaps it *is* a very serious one, depending upon your point of view). Far more vital might be the fact that there is not a petrol station or garage for miles. Or an hotel. Or even a tea-room. Tasmania is there to be explored – but in its way it needs to be treated with just as much care and respect as the Australian outback.

10 Queensland

If you want to know where the Murrisippi is, and are torn between somewhere in the American mid-west and the west coast of Australia, then the man to ask is a middle-aged former industrialist called John Longhurst. He knows all about this 800-metre long, 30-metre wide waterway. He ought to. He spent $2\frac{1}{2}$ years gouging out the man-made lake with a bulldozer.

The Murrisippi is the centrepiece of a new, $A13 million family entertainment complex at Coomera, on the Queensland coast, handily situated midway between the state capital of Brisbane and the rapidly growing resort area of Surfers Paradise. There is nothing else like it in Australia – and Australian holidaymakers are just beginning to discover it with a mixture of delight and incredulity. One day, quite soon, the development could be to Australia what Disneyland and Disneyworld are to the United States of America.

For John Longhurst it is a dream come true – a dream that he had on a flight between Hawaii and Japan after a trip to the United States during which he visited a number of the theme and entertainment parks which abound in that nation. He calls his dream, aptly enough, Dreamworld – and Dreamworld is one of the go-ahead ideas that is rapidly turning Queensland into both Australia's boom state and its top holiday destination.

It is a 208-acre entertainment complex which, in the best tradition of the American theme parks, offers its customers a mixture of fantasy and fun. A Mississippi-style paddle steamer churns its way around the lake with up to 250 passengers on board; a steam train trundles its way around the park; there are shops and shooting galleries, car rides and flume rides; restaurants and bars; a cinema in which the screen is so huge that viewers feel they are taking part in, rather than just watching, the action; and all the fun of the fair.

Queensland

Whooping cowboys sometimes emerge from the bush to hold up the train, and they may even search a passenger or two at gunpoint before disappearing back into their lair. Add the distinctly Western appearance of the surrounding buildings, and at first glance Dreamworld is a straightforward copy of its American forefathers. But on the other side of the Murrisippi, the restoration of an early Australian township is taking place. Koala bears snooze in the gum trees. John Longhurst's dream may have been born of what he saw in the United States of America, but he is an Australian first and let no one forget it. Dreamworld has an air about it which places it at least in the mid-Pacific, if not actually in Australia itself.

Dreamworld is of interest partly because it is an Australian success story. John Longhurst started out in life as a fitter and machinist, built up a motor mower business, turned that business into an empire, sold it, and then started up an entirely new project by manufacturing power boats. He made his millions, moved to Coomera with his family, ignored the critics and the sceptics, and started Dreamworld. And when he could not find anyone else prepared to dig out the lake that was to be the centrepiece of the project, he bought a bulldozer and did it himself. It was, he says, the hardest work he had ever done in his life. But the hole was eventually dug, filled with water, and christened the Murrisippi. American and Australian architects did the rest, and Dreamworld became a reality. Today it can hold up to 10,000 visitors at any one time, and has an expectancy of a million visitors a year – no mean achievement in a nation of 15 million people. Entrance fees are fairly high, but all the rides are free and some of them are really hair-raising. Some of the attractions are, admittedly, a trifle kitsch, and most of the souvenirs on sale are even more so. But the park provides a fun-packed day out for every member of the family.

The project is also of interest because it epitomises much of what is happening to this, the second largest Australian state, and particularly to its sub-tropical coastline. With typical gusto and flair, the Queenslanders are turning large areas of the coast into what will shortly become (if they have not already done so) Australia's leading holiday resort areas. True, not every development is as tasteful as one might wish, but then Queensland does have plenty of coastline to spare, and the farther north one travels the less frenetic the developments become.

Cross the border from New South Wales on the coast, at Tweed Heads, and you come quickly to Coolangatta, which is just inside

Queensland

Queensland and houses the airport which now mainly serves Surfers Paradise, 42 kilometres to the north. It also serves the string of attractive little resorts along the intervening coastline, which is known as the Gold Coast: resorts which are little more than villages, but which bear evocative, memorable names like Burleigh Heads, Miami, Mermaid Beach, and Broad Beach.

Ahead of you loom the skyscrapers of Surfers Paradise – known, universally, as 'Surfers', and the Miami Beach of Australia. In the context of Australia, Surfers Paradise is an anachronism. It is noisy, garish and brash. It is, relatively speaking, expensive. Its beaches, in a land of beaches, are crowded. Its buildings, in a country where land can hardly said to be in short supply, tower ever higher, almost – but not quite, because of a 'breathing spaces' planning policy – shouldering against one another on the shore. Buildings which are not skyscrapers face a future in which they are likely to be torn down, and replaced by another tower block of apartments or a tall, featureless hotel. Surfers Paradise and the adjoining Gold Coast attract $2\frac{1}{2}$ million holidaymakers every year. The great question is: why?

Local tourism officials cannot answer that. In fact, as long as the tills keep ringing, it must be doubtful whether they will stop to ask themselves the question. In 1960, Surfers Paradise was simply a little village to the south of Brisbane, with a rather nice beach. Because it was on a sand bar, with the Nerang River meandering along a few hundred metres behind the sea but parallel to it, it did bear a remarkable physical resemblance to Miami Beach, but surely that it is not enough to explain its rapid rise to fame and fortune. 'It just sort of caught on,' said one official vaguely. 'Word got around.'

What seems to have happened is that one or two apartment blocks were built there, and the citizens of New South Wales and Victoria decided that this was their chance to snap up a reasonably accessible (and, at that time, reasonably priced) holiday home in the sun. Friends, relatives and neighbours followed suit – and, quite suddenly, Surfers Paradise was the 'in' place.

Today, it has accommodation for 12,000 people, and that figure is increasing at the rate of 2000 or 3000 a year. People fall over themselves to buy either an apartment or a 'share' in an apartment which they can use for a week or two every year. One local firm sold $A1000 million-worth of property in one year in Queensland recently, most of it on the Gold Coast. The tourism business is already worth $A133 million a year to the region, and that figure is

25 Fossicking on the Great Barrier Reef at Heron Island, Queensland.

26 Underwater wonderland: Marineland, Green Island, Queensland.

27 Australia's answer to Disneyland: Dreamworld, near Brisbane, Queensland.

28 Just palm trees, sun and sand: Dunk Island, Queensland.

29 Rented yachts sail the Whitsunday Passage off the Queensland coast.

30 Victoria Bridge in Brisbane, state capital of Queensland.

31 Weird rock formations at the base of Ayers Rock, Northern Territory.

32 Aerial view of Ayers Rock, Northern Territory: the world's largest monolith.

33 The Olga Mountains: Ayers Rock's neighbours in the Northern Territory.

34 Aboriginal cave paintings can be found all over Australia, but especially in the Northern Territory.

35 The new skyline of Perth, capital of Western Australia, from the Swan River.

36 The baobab tree near Wyndham, Western Australia, whose hollow trunk was once used as a prison.

37 The strange rock formations of the Pinnacles, Western Australia.

Queensland

increasing rapidly. Property values are increasing rapidly too: the early investors in property in Surfers Paradise are now sitting on a fortune.

Perhaps surprisingly, those early buyers show little inclination to cash in on their investment by selling. They take their holidays there, or even retire there. They spend their mornings touring the pricey shops, and their afternoons improving on their suntans on the beach of fine white sand. Then, as the setting sun casts the long shadows of the skyscrapers over the beach, they retire to their apartments or hotel rooms to prepare for the cocktail hour and the long evening which stretches invitingly ahead of them – for Surfers Paradise is nothing if not a swinging spot, and the nightlife is varied. There is a big choice of restaurants, with the River Inn restaurant well worth a closer look; bars; and nightspots. The Chevron Hotel and the Surfers Paradise Hotel – both new, rather featureless edifices – are the only two licensed hotels, but the Chevron has a disco, and one can dine and watch a cabaret at Twains. There are four floors of entertainments at the Penthouse Club; youngsters may prefer to head for the Bombay Rock. If Surfers gets a casino, as it would like, its future will be secure. Or perhaps it is secure already: its way of life has certainly caught on, and it is able to attract top international cabaret stars.

Besides a casino, which would be a temptation to visitors from nearby New South Wales for whom such pleasures are banned, Surfers Paradise has its eyes on Australia's small boat boom, with plans for a couple of marinas, and on the world cruise market with plans to accommodate the largest ocean liners. It also knows that it serves as a useful overspill area for Brisbane, which is primarily a business centre and where accommodation is in relatively short supply. It points out, proudly, that despite its rapid development it is pollution free, and there is no oil on those glorious beaches. And it is not short of ideas for promotional gimmicks: its 'meter maid', a bikini-clad beauty whose job was to feed coins into parking meters so that motorists would not be booked, won worldwide fame.

Family entertainments are not forgotten, for despite its popularity with the older generation Surfers Paradise remains a family resort (70 per cent of its visitors are families) which expereinces an extraordinary crush during the midsummer Christmas holidays. There are cruises along the Nerang River and its maze of adjoining canals; lots of fishing trips; a wax museum; flights in vintage aircraft; horse shows, and trips to the Seaworld entertainment complex, which is rather like Dreamworld but puts the emphasis on waterborne exhibits and entertainments.

In fact, Surfers Paradise is an excellent starting point for longer excursions too, because behind the Gold Coast lies the lush countryside of the MacPherson mountain range: country which brochure writers like to describe as 'the green behind the gold'. This countryside makes a pleasant contrast to Surfers Paradise, for it is a mixture of rich dairy pastureland and thick rain forests. The green Numinbah Valley leads past the sheer face of the Springbook Spur, the wooded slopes of Lamington National Park, and the natural pools of the upper reaches of the Nerang River to the Natural Arch, where millions of litres of water thunder through a hole in the roof of a cave. Another route to the Springbrook Plateau passes a boomerang factory, where visitors can learn to throw the ancient aboriginal hunting stick (and, if they are lucky enough or skilful enough, get it back). On the waterfall-streaked Tamborine Mountain there is one of the world's few butterfly farms, and guests can stay in the attractive Binna Burra Lodge, on the edge of the national park. O'Reilly's Guest House is also recommended, and both are in excellent walking country.

Also inland, Korralbyn is building up a reputation as the area's most exclusive spot, and is known locally as the 'rich man's playground'. Perhaps the district's best day out, Dreamworld excepted, is to the Currumbin Sanctuary, which is run by the National Trust of Queensland. It is on the road south from Surfers Paradise, 500 metres south of Currumbin Creek Bridge, and there visitors can feed brilliantly coloured rainbow lorikeets, or wander among other indigenous wildlife such as kangaroos, wallabies, and koalas. And perhaps the region's most unnecessary excursion is to the Sunfun Tanning Centre, Chevron Island – where, according to the promotional literature, you can get that glowing, healthy look of the Gold Coast . . . safely and privately. Frankly, it would be cheaper on the beach.

With a permanent population of 100,000, Surfers Paradise is already Queensland's second largest city. But it is dwarfed by Brisbane, whose compact city centre and sprawling suburbs are home to nearly one million people – almost half the population of the state.

Compared with most Australian cities, Brisbane is curiously characterless. But it is also, in many ways, the most charming of the state capitals: it has, like Switzerland, an air of having come to terms

Queensland

with the twentieth century, and for the most part its people live – and enjoy – the good life. It stands slightly upstream on the Brisbane River, at the mouth of which, in Moreton Bay, the state's largest port is now being built. It is, of course, Queensland's principal commercial and industrial centre, boasting everything from a spaghetti factory to an oil refinery, and from a stock exchange to superb specialist shopping. It is also growing at a remarkable rate. Twenty years ago, the 92-metre high tower of City Hall was the tallest and best-known landmark in the city, but today that tower is dwarfed by a myriad of skyscraper office blocks and other high-rise buildings, while on the ground the suburbs spread ever farther afield.

The city looks its best from the Mount Coot-tha Lookout, in Mount Coot-tha Park just to the east of the city centre (the park also includes attractive Botanic Gardens). In the city itself, one feels slightly hemmed in by the skyscrapers, and by the apparent jumble of bridges (there are, in fact only a rail bridge and four road bridges, but they include the massive Captain Cook Bridge and four of the bridges are close together) crossing the Brisbane River. The centre of Brisbane stands on a sharp S-bend in the river, with another Botanic Gardens on one of the points – Gardens Point. In fact the city centre is almost ringed by parkland, but this does not camouflage the slightly claustrophobic atmosphere.

King George Square is at the heart of the city, and is dominated by the massive bulk of the City Hall which contains a collection of paintings and historic treasures. There is a good view of the city from the observation platform at the top of the clock tower. The city's other major building is the red-roofed, French Renaissance-style Parliament House; but visitors should also see the convict-built Observatory, in Wickham Terrace, which dates from 1829; the John Oxley Memorial obelisk, between Victoria Bridge and William Jolly Bridge, which marks the spot where Lieutenant John Oxley landed in 1823 and established the site of Brisbane; and Newstead House, the city's oldest residence (open daily from Monday to Thursday, and on Sunday afternoons). For a time during the Second World War, the American commander General Douglas MacArthur had his Pacific headquarters in Brisbane, and there is a United States memorial (dedicated to President Lyndon Johnson) in Newstead Park. Miegunyah, in Jordan Place, Bowen Hills, is a former colonial house, furnished in nineteenth-century style, and is open on Tuesdays and at weekends. Look out, too, for the Queensland Art Gallery, in Ann Street, which has a collection of works by contemporary Australian painters; and the Queensland Museum at the junction of Gregory Terrace and Bowen Bridge Road, which contains aboriginal artefacts and exhibits devoted to the Great Barrier Reef.

Good hotel accommodation is hard to find in Brisbane, and the most comfortable is probably Lennons Plaza Hotel – a modern property which mysteriously lacks good restaurant facilities, particularly at weekends. The Crest Motel is not bad, and has a good coffee shop. There are plenty of restaurants, however, with the Italian-owned Gambaro's – where you can eat shellfish until it is coming out of your ears, go on to a speciality main course like the local grilled barramundi fish, and still end up with a bill totalling less than half of what you would pay for a comparative meal in Britain, even supposing you could find one – being probably the pick of the bunch. Shopping is superb: there are several department stores, like David Jones and Myer's, as well as specialist gift shops specialising in local gemstones and native handicrafts from both Queensland and Papua New Guinea. Night-life is generally poor, although there is a Festival Hall, theatres, theatre-restaurants and a few discos. Queenslanders generally like a meal and a drink, or an evening at home in front of the television set.

One of the best excursions from Brisbane is to the Lone Pine Koala Sanctuary, a privately owned wildlife park on the banks of the Brisbane River and a two-hour boat trip or 20-minute drive from the city centre. The sanctuary was the first of its kind for koalas in Australia, and now has the largest collection of koalas on public display anywhere. You can have your photograph taken cuddling a koala – which makes a marvellous souvenir for the first-time visitor to Australia. The koalas have even been trained to ride on the back of a rather sheepish-looking alsatian dog. The sanctuary is worth spending a little time over: besides koalas it contains a collection of kangaroos, wallabies and emus – all perfectly tame and adept at rifling handbags and pockets for tasty titbits – and, if you show some enthusiasm for Australia's wildlife, the keepers may be persuaded to show you their duck-billed platypus, which is one of the very few in captivity but which is too highly strung to receive many visitors.

The Botanic Gardens in Mount Coot-tha Forest Park are impressive, and feature more than 2000 varieties of native and exotic plants in the tropical display dome. Besides excellent views of Brisbane and Moreton Bay, the Lookout takes in panorama which may extend as far as the Glasshouse Mountains, 80 kilometres away.

Queensland

Moreton Bay is also frequently visited, but is less interesting – although there are excursions to Moreton Island, at the mouth of the river, which contains the world's largest sand dunes (one, Mount Tempest, is 279 metres high), and to the beaches of Stradbroke Island.

North of Brisbane is another stretch of superb coastline, this time known as the Sunshine Coast. Less developed than the Gold Coast, the Sunshine Coast stretches from Caloundra (the principal resort) to Noosa Heads. Accommodation is a trifle limited, but the beaches are superb. Sunshine Beach, at Noosa Heads, is one of the world's top surfing beaches; and the cliff scenery around Noosa Heads is particularly fine, and contains such dramatic beauty spots as the Witches' Cauldron, Hell's Gates, the Devil's Kitchen, and Paradise Caves. It is also worth making an excursion to Kondalilla National Park, which has a fine waterfall, tropical rain forests, and numerous deep pools which are the home of that zoological oddity, the lung fish (see also Chapter 3).

The next feature of this coastline, travelling north, is the 145-kilometre long Fraser Island, which is excellent for all water sports. It is here that Queensland starts to take on a distinctly Polynesian atmosphere, which is accentuated by the popular Orchid Beach Village resort with its Samoan-style thatched hut accommodation. Inland, however, the scenery is still strictly agricultural: the farmlands of the Darling Downs and the 'garden city' of Toowoomba, a grain centre and Queensland's largest inland town. Toowoomba, incidentally, has a good Cobb & Co. Museum, which contains memorabilia of the days when transport in this vast land was by coach and horses – or on foot.

Deeper inland, the determined traveller will find the rolling sheep-farming lands around Roma, a town which has grown rich on wool and may yet grow richer on the natural gas and oil found there. North of Roma, the picturesque hills of the Carnarvon Ranges contain any number of aboriginal paintings and engravings on cliff faces and caves walls, left there by a people for whom this was once a popular hunting ground. It is not surprising that the hunters did well here, for the hills teem with wildlife. Travel even deeper into the southwest corner of the state, and you will come to the 'Channel Country' – land which gets its name from the network of channels which are formed there after the all-too-rare rainstorms. The town of Longreach is the gateway to the Channel Country, but beyond Longreach one is quickly into the outback, and a countryside that

Queensland

has an odd, primeval atmosphere despite the encroachment of civilisation and the twentieth century. Long road trains carrying stock to railheads and coastal markets, occasional tourist traffic, a few farmers, and aboriginal stockmen are one's only company in the huge, empty spaces. Visitors should look out for the Dig Tree at Cooper Creek, a coolibah tree beneath which the explorers Burke and Wills buried supplies for their ill-fated crossing of Australia in 1860 (Burke's likeness was carved on the tree in 1898); the hamlet of Birdsville, which is at the top of one of Australia's longest unmade roads, the Birdsville Track, leading all the way up from South Australia, but which has a population of only 80; and the cattle trucking centre of Winton. Winton has a proud place in both Australian history and Australian folklore. The nation's unofficial national anthem, *Waltzing Matilda*, was composed nearby by 'Banjo' Paterson in the early part of this century, while the little local airline that was born in the town, Queensland and Northern Territories Aerial Services, grew up to become Australia's famous international airline – still known by its initials, Qantas.

Australia is not particularly rich in ghosts or ghost stories. Perhaps the country is too young, or perhaps the people are too level-headed. But this region is also known for an unexplained phenomenon which is experienced by some travellers. At night, in the bush, a strange, dancing light is sometimes seen. It is called the Min-Min light. Nobody knows where it comes from or what causes it, but it certainly isn't man-made. But then, in the outback, you do get the feeling that you are at the mercy of nature and that anything could happen – and even the Min-Min is not totally unexpected.

All this is in dramatic contrast to the coastline, far away to the east. For Queensland's sub-tropical climate suddenly comes into its own around Nambour, and there are endless fields of pineapples (plus the man-made Big Pineapple). There are sugar cane and citrus fruits, too – and if you add these products to the rich pickings found by the coastal fishing fleets, the timber forests, the mines and the smelters, you begin to understand why Queensland is being looked upon as potentially one of Australia's two richest states (its only serious rival is Western Australia).

Much of Queensland's riches, however, are based on tourism, and that tourism is in turn based largely upon the state's accessibility to one of the world's greatest natural wonders, the Great Barrier Reef. The reef stretches north from Lady Elliot Island, south of the Tropic of Capricorn, right up the Queensland coast and across almost to the

Queensland

shores of Papua New Guinea – a total of just over 2000 kilometres. And it is a truly extraordinary attraction.

It is dotted with palm-studded coral islands just made for holidaymaking – among them the thickly wooded Heron Island just offshore from the town of Rockhampton, which is actually on the reef and is a skin-diving centre where turtles breed. Many other islands lie between the mainland and the reef, and although some are designated as national parks and are therefore protected, others have had hotels or holiday complexes erected on them. In some cases, these hotels are in dubious taste – a reflection, perhaps, of the fact that holidaymaking Australians, like holidaymakers the world over, put beer and beaches before beauty. Others, like the Royal Hayman Hotel on Hayman Island, are quietly luxurious. A few consist only of self-catering bungalow complexes. And all, as readers of Colleen McCullough's best-selling *The Thorn Birds* may remember, are extremely romantic.

Captain Cook discovered the Great Barrier Reef in 1770 – running the *Endeavour* on to the reef at one point. On Whitsunday of that year he sailed through what is now known as the Whitsunday Passage, between the mainland and the series of green-clad hills rising from the water which are the Cumberland, or Whitsunday, Islands. This is by far the most attractive group of islands off the Queensland coast: the islands look like the Greek islands or the islands off the west coast of Scotland, transplanted to the tropics. They lie just offshore from Proserpine, and north of Mackay, both towns which are linked to Brisbane by scheduled air services. There are boat services to the islands from both towns, as well as from the tiny and heart-rendingly pretty little port of Shute Harbour, right opposite the islands. Shute Harbour, apparently exceptionally well protected from the elements, looks like one of the most idyllic spots on this Earth, but it has a population of only about 60, most of them people who sail yachts, hire out yachts, or merely live on yachts. And that population suffered a tragic loss some years ago, when a tropical cyclone hit the harbour and one in ten of its population died trying to save their boats. Every earthly paradise, it seems, has its drawbacks.

Helicopters from Proserpine also fly across to Hayman Island, the most northerly of the Cumberland Isles, which is a green-topped hill peeping out of an azure sea and ringed by beaches of bright yellow sand. To call it the holiday island to end all holiday islands might sound like an exaggerated claim, but Hayman Island is certainly one of the loveliest and most peaceful spots that I have seen anywhere in

THE GREAT BARRIER REEF

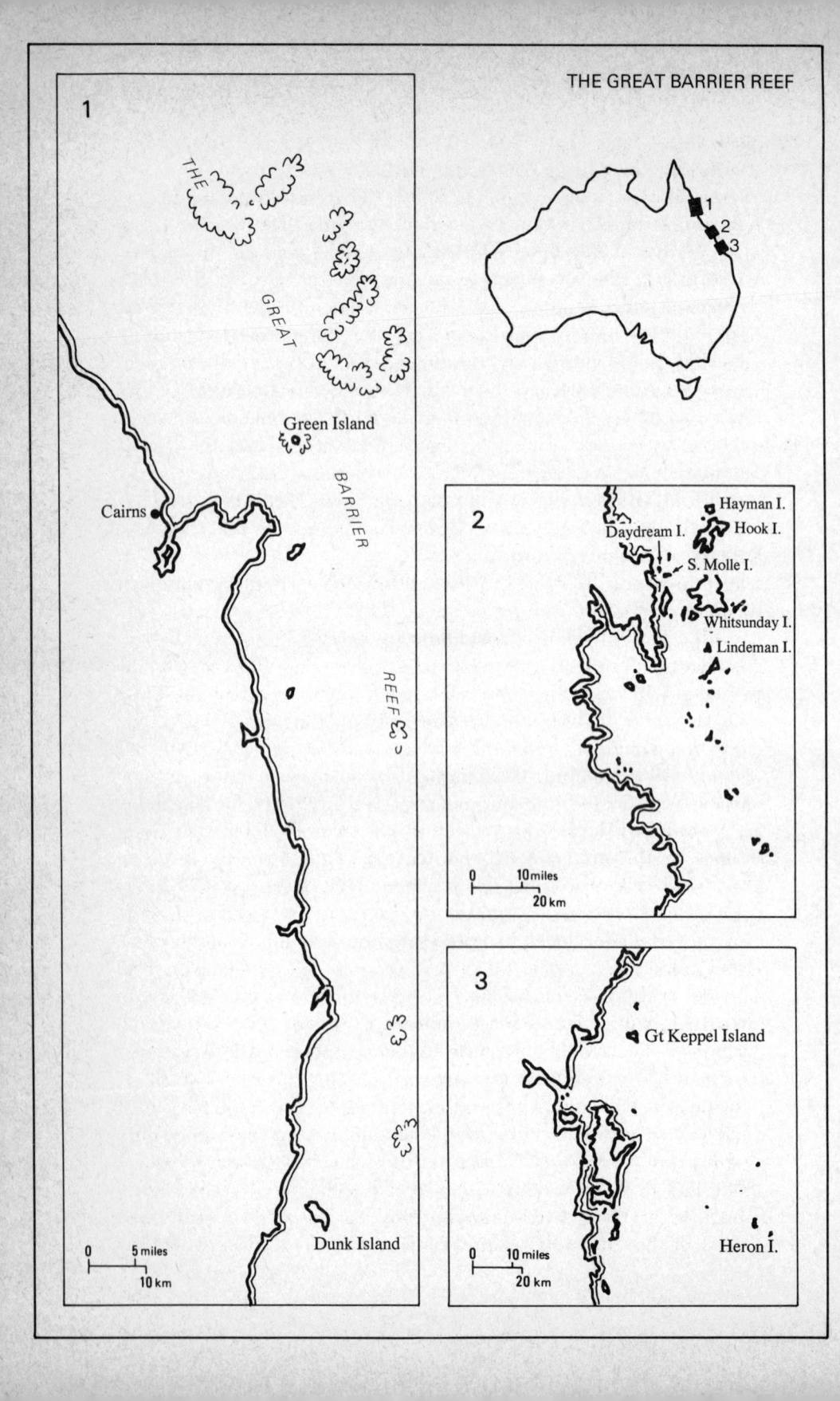

Queensland

the world, and André Maestracci, the extrovert Frenchman who runs the bungalow-style Royal Hayman Hotel, would certainly agree with me. He ought to know: he left Tahiti for Hayman Island, claiming that the Pacific paradise was passé.

The Royal Hayman Hotel (the 'Royal' was added by King George VI, who was meant to stay there but never quite made it) is a smart, efficient hotel with excellent facilities, and it also has something which its neighbours on other islands largely seem to lack: style. Its guests stay in bungalows or flats dotted around the wooded grounds, and as the hotel is the only development – indeed, the only major building – on the island, one's only neighbours are fellow guests and the noisy white parakeets which inhabit the treetops and sound their own, distinctly unmusical, dawn chorus. A little train puffs its way through the hotel grounds to the jetty, even though the latter is only a couple of hundred yards away, and there are nightly dances and cabaret shows in the ballroom. The latter tend to have a Polynesian flavour: a reminder that the boundless Pacific starts here.

You can inspect the neighbouring reef from the hotel's own glass-bottomed boat, or take a larger boat across to the nextdoor Hook Island, which has a fascinating underwater reef observatory. Or, for a modest fee, the aerial cowboys of Air Whitsunday will pick you up from the hotel beach in their flying boats and whisk you out to the main reef, 20 to 30 miles offshore. There you can sit in another glass-bottomed boat, moored to the reef, for half a day, or snorkel in the lukewarm water, or even walk (you need tennis shoes, as the coral is sharp) on the reef itself. And as you inspect this wonderland, you have to pinch yourself to see if it is real. The reef is a vast, open-air aquarium, inhabited – so the experts say – by up to 900 species of colourful fish and made up of hundreds of species of coral.

The reef has taken millions of years to build. It is made up of countless tiny anemone-like creatures, coral polyps, which secrete protective, distinctly patterned, limestone shells on the skeletons of their forefathers. Sharks and big turtles cruise outside the reef, but inside you will find nothing more dangerous than the occasional jellyfish in summer. The reef is a community on its own, with its own balance of nature. The latter was temporarily upset when, in recent years, the reef was invaded by hordes of crown-of-thorns starfish, which destroy the coral, and for a time the entire reef was thought to be in danger. Conservationists battled with the starfish,

Queensland

but were fighting a losing battle until the invader vanished as quickly and mysteriously as he had come, leaving behind nothing worse than a few gaps in the reef.

Excursion boats from Hayman Island and from the mainland tour Hook Island, the big Whitsunday Island which is now a national park, and the offshore Daydream Island, South Molle Island, and Long Island, all of which have their own, rather unattractive, tourist developments. Some tours even get down as far as romantic Lindeman Island, at the centre of the Whitsunday group, and attractive Brampton Island, the most southerly of the islands. There are also longer, mainland-based, four to five-day reef cruises, whose itineraries include calls at the major island resorts as well as a whole day spent fossicking (a verb which seems to mean 'exploring at a leisurely pace') on the Outer Reef.

Farther north, there are other island holiday centres from which the reef is easily accessible. Lizard Island, north of Cooktown and the most northerly resort in Queensland, is in game fishing waters just inside the Outer Reef, and has a small hotel and rather basic camping (the island is a national park). There are four islands off Townsville: Dunk Island, which is almost covered by thick tropical foliage but has a good hotel in the shape of the Great Barrier Reef Hotel; colourful Magnetic Island, just offshore, which is good for hiking; secluded Orpheus Island, which has some bungalow accommodation; and mountainous Hichingbrooke Island, which has palm-fringed beaches and good resort accommodation (it, too, is a national park). Green Island, off Cairns, is growing in popularity with tourists, and has an underwater observatory and lots of other opportunities to study the marine life of the reef. Great Keppel Island, far to the south and below the reef, off Rockhampton, is also an increasingly and justly popular holiday resort. On any of these islands, visitors straight from the city, and especially straight from Europe, should beware of sunburn: the tropical sun is hot, the air unpolluted, and you can burn in 15 or 20 minutes.

Many of the islands off the Queensland coast, as well as the adjacent mainland ports and towns, now feature in short-stay inclusive holiday programmes from Brisbane, and from major southern cities such as Sydney and Melbourne. Such a tour would be ideal for people visiting friends or relatives in Australia, and in need of a little side-excursion or sightseeing. Every visitor to Australia should try to see at least something of the Great Barrier Reef, for it is

Queensland

one of the most attractive and memorable spots anywhere in the country – and perhaps anywhere in the world.

The mainland cities, opposite the Great Barrier Reef are known as 'the gateway cities' – although in several cases the word 'city' is more than a trifle euphemistic. All have road, rail and air links with Brisbane.

Gladstone, 300 kilometres north of Brisbane, is the first of these, and is a busy, fast-growing cargo port built on the shores of the near-perfect natural harbour of Port Curtis. Despite the fact that much of the coal mined in Queensland passes through the port, it is an attractive town with an industrial atmosphere pleasantly tempered by the beautiful surroundings. Inland, at Mount Morgan, can be seen the vast, 250-metres deep open-cast mine out of which gold and copper have been dug for over a century. Some copper is still mined there, but the gold has gone and all that remains is the vast, corkscrew-shaped hole that is a reminder of the state's golden days.

Rockhampton is a fair-sized town of 54,000 people, and is known as the beef capital of Australia. It has been there for a long time, and retains many impressive colonial-style buildings as well as boasting excellent botanic gardens and a new civic centre which includes a theatre and an art gallery housing the city's famous collection of contemporary Australian paintings. As it is situated right on the Tropic of Capricorn, it just qualifies for the adjective 'tropical'. That means it can get very hot, and sea cruises, trips to Great Keppel Island, and sightseeing flights up to the reef by Country Air Services are all popular recreations.

A rather more unexpected recreation is shouting! Cooee Bay, northeast of Rockhampton, is setting for the World Cooee Championships in which contestants test out their lung power by shouting . . . well, you don't really need to be told what they shout, do you?

Nearby Yappoon is the site of a new multi-million dollar international tourist complex, while inland from Rockhampton amateur prospectors still hunt for buried treasure in and around the towns of Anakie, Sapphire, Rubyvale, the Willows and Tomahawk. Those who cannot find gems of their own can see what they missed in Rockhampton's gem and mineral centre, where the cutting, polishing and setting of gemstones is demonstrated and local gemstones and jewellery are on sale. Visitors should also visit charming Quay Street – the nineteenth-century ambience of which is emphasised by

Queensland

the occasional cowboy or stockman's hat bobbing among more conventionally-dressed shoppers, and there is good shopping in a variety of department and other stores. There is a full range of accommodation, up to surprisingly luxurious motels, and walkers will enjoy the trek through Carnarvon National Park to the ancient aboriginal tribal grounds and a brilliant display of cave paintings which date back thousands of years.

Mackay is an attractive, spacious, modern city with wide, palm-shaded streets and tropical flower gardens. Lying at the mouth of the Pioneer River, it shares with Rockhampton the advantages of a busy port – but this time the cargoes are sugar (Mackay's other name is the 'sugar capital' of Australia) and coal. As one might suspect, it is surrounded by cane-fields and coalfields – an often flat and rather dull panorama which makes the attraction of the Whitsunday Islands, to the north, even more pointed. Inland from Mackay, beyond the cane-fields, are the cool, jungle-like heights of Eungella ('the Land of Cloud') National Park, at the top of the Clark Range. Neighbouring Proserpine, directly opposite the Whitsunday Islands, is a tiny sugar town of only 3000 people. But it is full of exotic tropical flowers, and its flourishing links with the islands could put it, unexpectedly, on the holiday map itself one day soon.

Farther north still one comes to Townsville, third city of Queensland and, with a population of nearly 100,000, the largest tropical city in Australia. A dynamic industrial city, modern port, and important railway junction (the coastal line continues north to Cairns, while the Great Northern Railway travels inland, west to the copperfields of Mount Isa), Townsville is not exactly the sort of place which one would choose for a holiday. But it is surprisingly attractive, colourful and modern, with a smart city centre, unexpectedly good shopping and accommodation, and the lively atmosphere which one would expect of a university town. Many of the public buildings are new, including the futuristic civic centre. And Townsville is at the heart of an area which is worth a little exploring: there are lovely holiday islands, and the reef, offshore; while the Flinders Highway leads inland to Charters Towers, an historic town which once had the richest goldfield in Queensland (it peaked in 1899). Many of the original buildings from the gold-rush days still stand in Charters Towers, and these have been preserved and restored by the National Trust. Because it is in good pastoral country, the town has survived the demise of the goldfield; far from being a 'ghost town', it is flourishing.

Queensland

There is some spectacular scenery to be found inland, too – the tropical rain forests and rugged mountains of the Mount Elliot and Mount Spec national parks, and the 300-metre high Wallaman Falls (the highest sheer-drop falls in the state) on the Herbert River.

Finally, in this list of coastal cities, there is Cairns – a sort of frontier town which, almost to its own surprise, has become a popular winter holiday resort and a major game-fishing centre (the fishing, principally for black marlin, is excellent). Sportsmen like film star Lee Marvin fish there, hunting for the first 2000-lb fish for which there is a big prize. Cairns is a massive 1766 kilometres north of Brisbane, and is the entry point not only to the Great Barrier Reef and the ocean, but to the lush tablelands and untamed gulf country for which it is the commercial and industrial centre.

It is named after William Wellington Cairns, governor of Queensland from 1875 to 1877, and is a pretty city studded with tropical shrubs and flowers. A lot of the local attractions are aquatic (the House of 10,000 Shells, in Abbot Street; Cairns Reef World, on the Esplanade; Windows on the Reef, in Aumuller Street; and Cairns Crystal Cave), but there are also the exuberantly colourful Botanical Gardens, in which tropical foliage is combined with a series of salt and freshwater lakes to form a haven for wildlife. From the gardens, tracks lead up to Mount Whitfield, from which there are panoramic views of the city. An historic home, the House on the Hill (Kingsford Street, Mooroobool) has been turned into the town's most striking motel and restaurant.

West of Cairns is the 'Great Plateau' of the Atherton and Evelyn Tablelands, where dense rain forests compete for space with tobacco plantations and beef and dairy farms. The number of natural beauty spots in this region is extraordinary. Serene Lake Placid lies at the entrance to the grandeur of the Barron Gorge; and sugar cane fields surround the route to Freshwater Creek and the spectacular Crystal Cascades. There are rail excursions along the scenic route from Cairns to Kuranda, from which one sees Barron Gorge and the Stoney Creek Falls. There is a mining museum at Chillagoe, as well as the remnants of copper, lead and silver mines; and the Royal Arch Caves in the national park, through which there are tours twice daily, include Ryan Imperial Cave, with its numerous fossils, and the Donna Caves. Millstream Falls, near Ravenshoe, is thought to be the widest waterfall in Australia; the Millaa Millaa Falls is certainly among the most picturesque. Innot Hot Springs, 29 kilometres from Ravenshoe, is one of the country's few thermal

Queensland

springs; the cylindrical well of Hypipamee Crater is a strange natural phenomenon; and the much-photographed and ancient Curtain Fig Tree at Yungaburra has huge root formations like a giant curtain.

To the north of Cairns stretches the vast, untamed, and isolated Cape York Peninsula, an ancient aboriginal domain with a great heritage of primitive art. The coastal road runs through Palm Cove (where the Australian Bird Park is worth a visit), to Machan's Beach, Hartleys Creek (where there is a good fauna reserve), and Port Douglas to Mossman. Port Douglas, once a gold rush town, is today noted for its many good sea food restaurants, set amid palms and tropical plants, and day trips from Port Douglas go to the coral atolls of the Low Isles.

Mossman is a serene, pleasant, cane-growing town, and beyond it the countryside becomes rugged – the road twisting inland before turning back to the coast and to Cooktown, another nineteenth-century gold rush town with some fine old colonial buildings (one of which serves as an Historical Museum) remaining. The Captain Cook Monument, erected in 1886, commemorates Captain Cook's landing at Cooktown in 1770 to make repairs to the *Endeavour*, and the 'Endeavour Tree' and Granite Boulder mark the spot where *Endeavour* was repaired.

The road from Cairns continues north, through Laura and Coen, to the northernmost tip of the Australian mainland at Cape York, with a spur leading west to the bauxite mining port of Welpa. For the most part this is wilderness country, 1000 kilometres of sandy tracks that can be explored only by four-wheeled drive vehicles, fast-flooding creeks, giant anthills, aboriginal sites, swampland and jungle. There are a few isolated cattle stations, but much of the countryside has now been designated as national parkland – there are eight major parks, with a total area of 1,500,000 hectares.

The rocky tip of Cape York, however, is not the end of Australia. Beyond it, across the Torres Strait which was discovered in 1606 by the Spanish navigator Luis Vaez de Torres, are strewn the picturesque Torres Strait Islands. Thursday Island, with a population of only 2200 people, is the administrative centre of the islands, but for the most part the dark-skinned Torres Strait islanders still live as they did when Torres first came across them – fishing, farming, and seeding pearls. One day, perhaps, the Torres Strait Islands may become a major holiday destination – but that day is not yet. Their inaccessibility protects them, but so does the fact that there is so much else to see and do in Queensland.

Queensland

Below the western edge of the Cape York Peninsula, there is more cattle and mining country. The unexpected Gulflander railway, connecting the inland towns of Normanton and Croydon, might be thought to lead from nowhere to nowhere, but serves a useful commercial role besides being one of the world's most isolated railways. Karumba is a busy little fishing port, with fleets of prawn boats, and anglers hunting for the Gulf of Carpentaria's sporty (and tasty) barramundi fish. And deep inland lies a booming city which almost every visitor to Australia hears about, but very few indeed ever see: Mount Isa.

You hear of Mount Isa because it is the first recognisable point on the mainland crossed by flights to Australia from Europe and the Far East. Besides aircraft communications, and a Royal Flying Doctor base, Mount Isa – situated in dry, inhospitable highlands – has vast mining complexes. It is built on top of what may be the world's richest deposits of copper, silver, lead and zinc, and almost every resident is a miner or a miner's dependent.

People from more than 50 countries have taken part in the modern equivalent of the gold rush, and made their homes in Mount Isa, where there seem to be plenty of jobs. They make the town a cosmopolitan place, and it is a rich place too: it has many modern buildings, including a new civic centre. But you would still need a lot of perseverance to live there, even if one of the hazards which beset the early inhabitants has been removed. In the nineteenth century, the settlers were terrorised by an unusually warlike tribe of aboriginals, the Kalkadoon tribe. The natives were finally subdued in a bloody pitched battle with native police troopers near Cloncurry in 1884. Later, in 1923, a wandering prospector found the ore samples which began the Mount Isa boom. Today you will not find any Kalkadoon (although they do have an attractive park named after them) in 'the Isa' – but you will find a strong community spirit and generous, if informal, hospitality. The city of 27,000 is always pleased to see visitors – if a trifle surprised that they have found their way to what must be one of Australia's remotest towns.

Queensland's energetic tourism authorities sum up the attractions of the immense, exciting, and seemingly perpetually sunny state thus: 'Where can you stub your toe on a fortune, discover ancient tribal paintings, walk on the world's largest living thing, relax in a world famous resort and hear a yarn spun at a fair

143

Queensland

dinkum outback pub?' There are no prizes for getting the answer right. Queensland is Australia as you had always imagined it, and I for one believe that it has the potential to become, one day, the world's greatest holiday resort. But that, I hope, is not yet.

11 Northern Territory

Unlike the ancient Greek gods, the heroes of aboriginal folklore out in the empty heartland of Australia have a refreshing mortality about them.

Way back in the misty past, which the aboriginals so picturesquely refer to as 'The Dreamtime', the first, legendary Australians did share with their Greek counterparts a rather distressing ability to turn themselves into birds and animals – usually with some mischief in mind. Zeus used to do that too, of course – when he wished to devote his attentions to some young mortal maiden and didn't want Hera to know about it. But supposing Hera *had* found out: would she have clubbed Zeus to death? No, of course she would not; for Zeus was King of the Gods.

But, on the other side of the world, Kadumalu – a sort of aboriginal deity who was also known as 'The Kangaroo Man' because of an alleged ability to turn himself into that mysterious marsupial – was not so lucky. He committed some trivial sin (the details seem to be uncertain, but it certainly was not as much fun as Zeus's philanderings), and was doomed to a ritual death. An aboriginal woman executioner tracked him down, stabbed him twice, broke his nose, then clubbed him to death with the short, heavy, carved *nulla-nulla* stick which – boomerangs apart – is the aboriginals' favourite weapon.

And, should you doubt this story, you can see Kadumula to this day. At least, the aboriginals say that you can. For his likeness – his face gashed and wreathed in agony – can be found on the side of the Olga Mountains which, like Ayers Rock, rise abruptly from the flat, featureless desert 340 kilometres west of Alice Springs. Time and the elements have played strange tricks with these rocks, and Kadumalu has his hand clutched to the side of his head and his nose is indisputably broken.

Northern Territory

The story of Kadumalu is told by explorer John Dare, who runs three-day 'safari' trips out to Ayers Rock and the Olgas from Alice Springs in his superbly equipped, air-conditioned coach. John Dare, and others like him who venture out into the wilderness of the Northern Territory, have a deep knowledge of aboriginal folklore, and often an unusual ability to communicate with the wandering tribespeople too. Besides the story of Kadumalu, John Dare has many other such tales, and he can lead the visitor to the sacred caves where the aboriginals record their stories in a colourful picture language, as well as explaining how, in a featureless landscape, those stories of the Dreamtime people are related to individual trees, boulders . . . even the earth itself.

For an aboriginal to trespass on these sacred sites is to risk expulsion from the tribe and certain death, even today. And, faced with such deeply held convictions, the Australian authorities are powerless to intervene. But non-aboriginals, it seems, are exempt from such strictures, so visitors can explore the wilderness at will.

And what a wilderness. The Northern Territory – it is not yet a fully fledged state, although it has aspirations in that direction, and is ruled from Canberra – comprises nearly one-sixth of Australia. It is roughly 1600 kilometres from north to south, and 930 kilometres from east to west. Yet in that vast area there are only two towns of note: Darwin, the territorial capital on the north coast, and Alice Springs at the geographical centre of the continent.

Darwin is a modern town of 25,000 people which has recovered well both from the Japanese bombs which fell on it during the Second World War and the assorted cyclones which have hit the city and surrounding areas. Indeed, Darwin is at the heart of a cyclone belt, and has already been hit three times in its history: in 1897, 1937 and 1974. But it seems to accept the danger stoically, and the wounds are not apparent – the city, built on the eastern shore of Port Darwin, is well planned and neatly laid out with tree-lined streets and attractive parks. The damage caused in 1974 has largely been repaired.

Darwin and the northern part of the territory are, of course, tropical. Known collectively as 'the Top End', they have only two seasons: 'the Wet' (November to April) and 'the Dry' (May to October). The latter is the only really practical time to visit Darwin, as 'the Wet' can be exceedingly hot and sticky as well as being studded with torrential tropical storms, which flood creeks and roads and cut off large areas.

Northern Territory

Because of its accessibility to South-East Asia, Darwin is an important commercial centre. Its strategic importance was recognised by the Japanese during the Second World War, and – although most of Australia was, fortunately, beyond the range of Japanese aircraft – a number of bombing raids were made on the city. It is logical to suppose that, if they had succeeded in invading Australia, the Japanese might have made their initial landings in Darwin, too – although where they would have gone next is highly questionable. The remains of the city's wartime defence installations can still be seen on East Point, where there is an artillery museum.

During 'the Dry', Darwin is an ideal swimming, sunbathing and sailing centre, and there are good beaches of silver sand at Mindil, Casuarina and Dripstone. Deep-sea fishing is also growing in popularity. The 14-acre Botanical Gardens feature tropical plants; while at Yarrawonga Park, 21 kilometres southeast of the city centre, there is a small zoological gardens containing some of the fauna of the Northern Territory – including dingos, emus, buffalos, and a variety of snakes. Shopping in the town itself, especially for aboriginal products, is reasonable.

The Northern Territory has a slightly odd taste in sporting activities – as is demonstrated by the famous Henley-on-Todd Regatta held in Alice Springs each year, when boats 'race' on the dried-out-bed of the Todd River. Whether the competitors are laughing at British institutions, suffering from a touch of the sun, or exercising their own dry sense of humour has long been open to question, but two events held in Darwin each June suggest that the latter is the case. One is the Northern Territory Walkabout (a reference to the aboriginal habit of disappearing for weeks or months on end while they 'go walkabout' in the bush), a 26-kilometre walking race open to all-comers. The other is the Beer Can Raft Regatta, at Mindil Beach, when craft made entirely of beer cans compete in various races. Rumour has it that more energy goes into creating the raw material from which the boats are made – i.e. empty beer cans – than into constructing the vessels themselves, but some entries are extraordinarily sophisticated and seaworthy craft.

The countryside around Darwin is unexpectedly attractive, and teeming with wildlife in its natural state. There are some oddities to be seen too: the 'magnetic anthills' at Berry Springs and Howard Springs, south of the city, are huge mounds of mud built by white termites and always constructed on a precise north-south axis. At the Fogg Dam Bird Sanctuary, 58 kilometres southeast of Darwin,

Northern Territory

thousands of birds gather to produce an ear-shattering dawn chorus, while wild buffalos live on the surrounding plains.

But the most famous beauty spot is probably Katherine Gorge, near the town of Katherine 354 kilometres south of Darwin on the metalled highway (an advantage of the territory having been able to call on federal funds) which leads south and, eventually, to Alice Springs 1530 kilometres away. Here, boats journey along the Katherine River between 60-metre high canyon walls decorated with aboriginal paintings. There are also a number of walks through the park. 'Safari' trips into the bush are also available from Darwin, and although the surrounding countryside does not makes these as exciting as those from, say, Alice Springs, the trip to western Arnhemland, rich in wildlife, is worth doing.

The wildlife of the Northern Territory is, incidentally, stringently protected. This has not always been the case, as many of the aboriginal rock paintings in which the territory is so rich clearly demonstrate. These depict kangaroo hunts and other tribal activities, as well as X-ray-type paintings showing both the internal and external features of men and animals. It is to be hoped that these paintings – which have not yet been fully catalogued, and indeed not all of which may by any means yet have been discovered – will be preserved as assiduously as Australia's wildlife.

Alice Springs, or simply 'The Alice', lies 'down the track' from Darwin, a green but not particularly attractive oasis in the heart of Australia's 'Red Centre'. It has earned international fame partly as the subject of Nevil Shute's best-selling novel, *A Town Like Alice*, and partly because it is, almost literally, a thousand miles from anywhere else of note. But if anyone thinks that the world's more out-of-the-way spots must necessarily be romantic places, then Alice Springs may well disappoint them. It is an ugly little town, full of tin-roofed bungalows, short on amenities, and plagued by flies. If you have ever wondered why the archetypal Australian bushman is portrayed wearing a hat with corks dangling on strings from the brim, the Alice's clouds of flies will provide you with an answer. The flies even give rise to what the locals call 'the Alice Springs salute' – a perpetual waving of the hand in front of the face to keep the flies away from your mouth, nose and eyes. With even grimmer humour, the locals also insist that you can tell how long anyone has been in Alice Springs by watching his reaction to the flies. 'People who have been in Alice for one day brush the flies off their faces', explained one resident. 'People who have been here for two days brush the flies off

Northern Territory

their food. And after three days, people ignore the flies altogether.'

Add to the flies and the remoteness of the place the fact that Alice Springs seems to have only two kinds of weather – hot (in winter) and extremely hot (in summer) – plus occasional rainstorms which can cut off the place from the rest of the world altogether, and one might begin to wonder why Alice Springs is there at all. The answer is that it was born in 1872 when a telegraph repeater station on the trans-Australia line was established near a waterhole christened Alice Springs after the wife of the superintendent of telegraphs, Charles Todd. Never can such an unassuming couple have given so much of their identity to a place: the local river, which is usually bone dry, was named after Todd himself.

After the Second World War, the hamlet, as it was until then, grew up as a commercial and market centre for the remote farms and cattle stations for hundreds of miles around, rather in the manner described in *A Town Like Alice*. And today it is a wealthy town of 16,000 people; it is growing fast; and because of its relative proximity to Ayers Rock it has become a tourist attraction. Surrounded by bare red hills, it has been carefully laid out, and it has become almost a cult place. A small bungalow in Alice Springs would cost you as much to buy as a similar property on the outskirts of Sydney or Melbourne, or a small house in the London suburbs. This is largely because many government offices and firms in Australia require representation in the Alice, and pay additional allowances to staff who are posted there. The demand for property, and prices, have risen accordingly.

Although the sea is 1320 kilometres away at its nearest point, Alice Springs reminds one vaguely of a seaside town: it has the same wide streets, shaded shop-fronts, and limitless horizons. There is more to see and do than might at first be supposed – although all the local sights can easily be covered in a couple of days.

From the tiny airport, from which there are several flights a day to and from Adelaide, the road leads through a gap in the featureless hills to the suburban sprawl of Alice itself, and one's first stop should be at the war memorial on Anzac Hill, from which there is a panoramic view of the city. You can get your bearings from Anzac Hill, but to be honest the panorama is far from exciting. Alice Springs is short on eye-catching features.

It is fairly short on history, too. The Old Telegraph Station, three kilometres from the town centre and in service until 1932, has been restored and contains a museum, and is a popular tourist venue

Northern Territory

standing in national park land (open daily). It has a rather fort-like appearance, which it acquired of necessity when the local aboriginals took umbrage and attacked it. But the Old Telegraph Station is perhaps the one place in Alice Springs in which, today, one can begin to appreciate the dangers and the hardship which were endured by the early settlers (and, indeed, the not-so-early settlers; even in 1927 the town had a white population of only 40). It is an empty, haunted place – a place which, like the vast empty spaces beyond the confines of Alice Springs itself, has a timeless, ethereal quality about it which the aboriginals have always understood and which a few enthusiastic (and usually young) settlers are only now beginning to appreciate. The aboriginals are at one with their environment – and in the Red Centre of Australia one begins to get a glimmer of understanding of this philosophy.

The aboriginals are not at one with city life. Alice Springs has its fair share of them, and every visitor will see them sleeping in the parks or chatting quietly in groups beneath a roadside eucalyptus tree. They do not mix much with the European latecomers to the Alice, and the feeling is mutual. Some settlers are at the same time patronising and contemptuous. 'The aboriginals', explained one white local, 'are the only race in the world never to have contributed anything to civilisation. They have never invented anything, never done anything.' The rock paintings all over Australia belie this claim, for the aboriginals undoubtedly have – and in country areas still have – their own civilisation: incomprehensible to us, perhaps, but also uncomprehending of many aspects of European civilisation. You can get an odd feeling about those aboriginals, sitting quietly and patiently under the trees in the Westernised centre of Alice Springs. You can get the feeling that they are waiting for you, and everyone else, and everything that has grown up there in the past 40 or 50 years, to go away.

If the aboriginals have such thoughts, however, it is unlikely that they are conscious ones. The aboriginals have benefited more than anyone else from two of the services which have their headquarters in Alice Springs: the Royal Flying Doctor Service, and the School of the Air.

In many ways, the Royal Flying Doctor Service's base, in Stuart Terrace, is Alice Springs' grandest building – complete with its official insignia adorning the frontage. The base is open to tourists on weekdays and on Saturday mornings, and visitors are treated to a short audio-visual and lecture about the work of the Royal Flying Doctor Service as well as being able to eavesdrop on simulated consultations between patients in the outback and the base. Even if you could eavesdrop on an actual consultation, the patient probably would not mind – for in the outback two-way radio receivers are often kept switched on as they form remote homesteads' only means of communication with the outside world. As a result, everyone knows everyone else's business.

Although it treats no patients on the spot (the town's hospital is nearby), the base has something of the air of a hospital about it. In fact, one is almost disappointed not to find doctors, carrying their little black bags, dashing to waiting planes and taking off to deliver a baby on some remote cattle station. The reality is rather more prosaic than that. All but the most serious illnesses are 'treated' over the radio, with the base's staff perhaps diagnosing the patient's symptoms and prescribing treatment from the comprehensive medical supplies with which every homestead, cattle station or mining camp in the outback is equipped. Only in the most serious cases – an aboriginal stockman injured in a fall, perhaps, or an accident at a mining camp – is the doctor called in.

In fact, there is not even a doctor at the base: he is at the hospital. He, or one of his staff, presides over daily 'surgeries of the air', which are held morning and afternoon. During these surgeries, the 1000 people in the outback linked to the service can call the base, using an individual call sign, and seek advice. After 5 p.m., when the base closes down, the doctor can still be contacted by radio in an emergency. But he rarely flies out to his patients these days – rather, an ambulance plane (paid for by the Northern Territory) flies out and brings the patient back to his hospital in Alice Springs. The majority of patients are aboriginals.

The radios cost $A1400 each, have a range of about 2000 kilometres, and are not used only for medical emergencies. They can be linked into the national telephone service, and they are also widely used for sending telegrams ordering food or fuel supplies. These orders are received by the Royal Flying Doctor Service in Alice Springs, and the telegrams are passed to the post office for onward transmission. The radios use four frequencies, one of which is kept free for emergencies. One shorter-range frequency is used by people in the outback simply for 'chatting' with the neighbours, who may be 100 kilometres or even 500 kilometres away. It is odd to listen-in to one of these apparently trivial, gossipy chats – and even odder to think that 500 other people may be listening in! There's no talking about the neighbours – and swearing is banned.

Northern Territory

There are now 11 other Flying Doctor bases like the one in Alice Springs, covering two-thirds of the Australian continent. Outside Alice, the most famous are at Kalgoorlie, in Western Australia; Broken Hill in New South Wales; and Charleville, Cairns and Mount Isa in Queensland.

An extension of the Royal Flying Doctor Service is the School of the Air, which now has its own headquarters in northern Alice Springs. This is aimed at the children in the outback, who are taught by a combination of correspondence units and radio 'lessons' during which the teacher can address each child by name, comment on his or her work, and answer any questions. 'For the children, it is just like being in the classroom except that there is no teacher actually there in the room with you', explained one official. The School of the Air started off by teaching 20,000 children living in remote parts of the Northern Territory, but the idea has recently spread to country areas of Queensland and Western Australia too. The School of the Air is open to visitors on weekday afternoons, and tourists can listen in to actual lessons.

Both the Royal Flying Doctor Service and the School of the Air help the visitor to realise the enormity of the region of which Alice Springs is the centre. Rather more space-shrinking is Alice Springs' only other real tourist attraction, the Panorama Guth. This is a gallery in which a huge, 61-metre long circular painting of the landscape around Alice Springs can be viewed from a special platform. The painting is by a Dutch artist, Henk Guth, and in an attempt at realism the painting has been carefully lit and given a 'foreground' of sand and shrubs which give it a three-dimensional effect.

The Panorama Guth is the pride of Alice Springs' tourism officials, but I found it both ugly and misleading. The painting leads one to believe – unintentionally, no doubt – that from, say, Anzac Hill one should be able to see the geological wonders of the surrounding countryside, like Ayers Rock, the Olgas, or Ormiston Gorge. In Australian terms, no doubt, these features are close to the town; but they are far beyond the limits of human vision.

Far closer to town is the Emily Gap Camel Farm, on the edge of Alice Springs, which is an amusing spot on the tourism map for visitors. Once, camel trains were the principal means of supply to Alice Springs, the camels having been imported during the nineteenth century. Today, most of the camels have been turned loose, and have found a home in the Australian desert. But a few remain in

Northern Territory

captivity, and the Emily Gap Camel Farm has a large herd of these. The beasts are used to carry camping safaris into the outback, but visitors to the farm can take a far shorter ride around a dusty paddock, clutching wildly at the animal's hump as it wavers its way along. They say you can get seasick if you ride for long on 'the ship of the desert' – and I can believe it! Besides being ungainly, the camel is an untidy-looking and ill-tempered beast: the careless or foolhardy human who wanders too close to one can be spat at or bitten. But the camel has none the less become a part of the Australian outback, and for that reason, if for no other, the Emily Gap Camel Farm is worth a visit.

The residents of Alice Springs have created for themselves a fairly lively social life, which includes excellent sporting facilities and a lot of entertaining. But, despite its apparently transient nature, the community is a close-knit one. Somehow, the visitor never seems comfortable there. Hotels and motels are expensive in relation to what they offer for your money, which is not much, and perhaps it is only after you have been in the outback for a few days that you really come to appreciate them. The Oasis Motel is perhaps the best, but do not expect five-star luxury, and do expect somewhat basic meals. There are good meals to be found in and around Alice Springs, but you need to ask local advice to track them down. One or two of the town's pubs, for example, serve excellent lunches in cool, air-conditioned comfort; while there are enterprising young couples opening restaurants like the Chateau Hornsby, just outside the town and featuring dinner beneath open skies and the Southern Cross. The only trouble with such outdoor places is that you will be joined for dinner by hordes of nocturnal insects, and although the proprietors may well have installed one of those oddly coloured lamps which kill insects, dining to the sound of large moths electrocuting themselves is distinctly unromantic.

Shopping is surprisingly good in Alice Springs – surprisingly, that is, until one remembers that it is the only shopping centre for a thousand miles in any direction. Despite the heat, the shops keep normal European hours, but they do close for the weekend at lunchtime on Saturday. Prices can be high because of transport costs. The best buys for tourists, probably, are aboriginal arts and crafts.

Alice lets its hair down three times a year, with three of the oldest activities to be found anywhere in Australia. The first of these local festivals is in May, when the Bangtail Muster is staged. This dates

Northern Territory

back to the old cattle round-ups, and although there are not many cattle in evidence at the event these days it does include a procession and sporting events. Next, in late August, comes the town's most famous event, the Henley-on-Todd Regatta. Although the River Todd 'flows' through Alice Springs it is almost always bone dry, but this does not stop the town's younger and more energetic citizens from staging a full-scale regatta on it, complete with skiff, yacht and canoe races, and an annual international 'Australia Cup' battle between yachts representing Australia and the United States. All the boats, one must hasten to add, have no keels to them, and are propelled by the leg power of their occupants. And if you find that eccentric, then just wait for the Camel Cup in September, a day at the races but with camels replacing horses – for there is nothing more eccentric than a haughty camel with lots of bets resting on its performance but a firm disinclination to go anywhere at a walk, let alone at a run.

The camels of Alice Springs, or rather their original Afghan drivers, inspired the name of the once-a-week train which since 1929 has run between Adelaide and Alice Springs: the Ghan. In a way, the Ghan ended Alice's isolation, but the rail journey could be nearly as heart-breaking as the road journey up from Adelaide on dirt roads. The old railway planners picked the easiest route, and unfortunately failed to notice that in several places the track crossed river beds or salt flats which were liable to flooding after storms. What was supposed to be a 36-hour journey was sometimes halted (usually at a handily situated track-side pub), while the track was relaid, and on one memorable occasion the Ghan arrived in Alice Springs a record three months late. Recently the line has been rerouted to avoid these wet season pitfalls, and a new train – the 'New Ghan' – now makes the journey in 24 hours. What is more, the line is to be extended up to Darwin very shortly, which will effectively open up vast regions of central Australia to tourism as well as removing much heavy commercial transport from the roads.

One gets a taste of what roads can be like in the Australian outback quite close to Alice Springs, for on most excursions out of town the asphalt surface soon gives way to a track of red dust which coats vehicles with ochre, dries your throat, and reflects the heat until you feel as though you are driving through a furnace.

But the tourist sights in the region are worth the discomfort. The 150-metre high gorge of Simpson's Gap, 19 kilometres west of Alice Springs, is the closest to town; Standley Chasm, 53 kilometres west

Northern Territory

of Alice, is rather more spectacular; and the canyon of Palm Valley, 145 kilometres west of Alice and dotted with groves of ancient palm trees, is an unexpected oasis. But the high spot of a westward drive is undoubtedly Ormiston Gorge – Australia's Grand Canyon. Ormiston Gorge is neither as long nor as deep as the Grand Canyon, but its towering red and purple rock walls overlooking pools of water (or, if it has been raining, the raging torrent of Ormiston Creek) probably make it more spectacular. Its sheer remoteness means that relatively few people have seen it, or perhaps even heard of it, but one day Ormiston Gorge will be one of the principal tourist destinations in Australia.

Ayers Rock and the Olgas already are major tourist destinations. You can reach them by plane from Alice Springs (there are daily scheduled services), or by road on one of the safari-type excursions mentioned earlier. They lie to the southwest of the town, and they are extraordinary because of their size and the abruptness with which they rise from the flat landscape which surrounds them.

They are also extraordinary because, according to geologists, they are among the oldest rocks in the world: all that remains of a massive mountain chain which once stood in the flat, featureless countryside.

Ayers Rock, rearing out of the desert like the back of some immense, sleeping prehistoric monster, is made of sandstone and is 348 metres high and $8\frac{1}{2}$ kilometres in circumference – and the largest monolith in the world. It is a place of mystery, of legend (features of the rock have been given names, such as the Skull), and of very considerable beauty. If you could take a series of photographs of the rock from sunrise to sunset – which is exactly what many photographic enthusiasts go there to do – you would see that it changes colour from yellow to gold, then to its natural red, and finally passes through an ever-deepening series of reds to purple.

Coaches make the circuit of the rock at ground level, and tracks leading off the dirt road go through the scrub to secret pools and caves which are aboriginal holy places and many of which contain rock and cave paintings. The rock itself is, perhaps surprisingly, not considered a holy place by the aboriginals – who called it 'Uluru'. But it does have a very odd atmosphere, made odder when one recalls that 100 years ago its existence was not known to Australia's European settlers. Today, the hardy (perhaps one should say the foolhardy) can climb to the top of the rock, but despite the erection of a handrail this is extremely difficult and can be dangerous as the surface is very slippery. It looks easy, but you need to be properly

Northern Territory

shod, and the climb can take several hours. The record for the climb (held by a New Zealand athlete) is 12½ minutes. A less enviable record held by the rock is that it claims two or three fatalities every year – for if you slip and fall on the rock there is nothing to stop your downward progress until you hit the bottom.

There are several very scruffy motels in the vicinity of the rock, as well as camping sites. The former have been allowed by their owners to decay because the authorities could not decide what development they would or would not allow in the Ayers Rock area, but it has now been decided that a tourist village should be developed at Yulara, 14 kilometres west of the rock. As this gets under way, together with the building of a rather more formal airport (until recently the airport consisted of a runway and a caravan), the accommodation will undoubtedly improve beyond all recognition, for Ayers Rock is undoubtedly a sufficiently popular tourist destination to attract considerable investment.

The Olgas, another group of more than 30 dome-shaped sandstone monoliths separated by deep ravines, lie about 32 kilometres west of Ayers Rock. They may not be as dramatic as Ayers Rock, but they are higher (Mount Olga, the highest point, rises to 549 metres), and they are certainly more attractive.

Coach tours tend to stop for lunchtime picnics and barbecues in the lightly wooded countryside at the foot of the Olgas, where a passing kangaroo may stop inquisitively to watch you eat. The ravines are worth exploring, as well as providing welcome shade, while the Olgas themselves can be climbed by the easy Kata Juta route. The path is well marked and well trodden, and even if the going is sometimes steep the views from the top are stunning.

But make sure that you are back at Ayers Rock in plenty of time for the sunset: for otherwise you will miss the most extraordinary show that I have ever seen put on by Mother Nature. John Dare stops his coach at a local vantage point, and magically produces from the door in the side of his vehicle a set of glasses and a cocktail shaker. Sipping a martini in one of the world's most out-of-the-way spots as the sun dips below the horizon and Ayers Rock changes from deep red to purple and then to black is one of the most unforgettable sights that one could find anywhere.

And if the strength of those martinis ensures that you miss that other show a few hours later, at dawn – well, never mind. For an all-to-brief moment in time you will have glimpsed and felt something of what this, the world's oldest continent, is all about.

12 Western Australia

Western Australia is a state so large that one blinks over the statistics – or perhaps does not take them in at all. It covers 2·6 million square kilometres, or a million square miles, and with a population of just about one million people that means an awful lot of room in which to move about. In fact, 80 per cent of the people live in an around the capital, Perth – so one can see just how sparse is the population of the rest of the state. Yet that state is bigger than Western Europe, or South Africa, or India.

Perth is an extremely attractive city, built on the lower reaches of the wide Swan River and likely to come second only to Sydney in any all-Australian beauty contest. And if, when you are there, you occasionally feel that you are somehow standing on the edge of the world – well, you are. Separated from the rest of Australia by the Nullarbor Plain in the south, and by deserts in the centre and north of the country, Perth stands very much on its own – and perhaps the most surprising thing about it is that it still manages to be a part of, even a pace setter for, modern Australia. Its nearest neighbour of any size is Adelaide, 2713 kilometres away by road. Singapore and Sydney are roughly equidistant from Perth.

If Perth, despite these drawbacks (or perhaps, as some would have it, these advantages), exudes a rather jaunty self-confidence, it might be due to the fact that things seem to be going Perth's way. The city fathers have every reason to believe that they have created almost ideal living conditions in the form of a state capital with a lovely setting, a Mediterranean climate, and no heavy industry to mar the horizon or cloud the atmosphere (all such heavy industry has been banished to Kwinana, down the coast). The state of Western Australia is already very rich, and potentially a lot, lot richer – for the western half of the state is thought by most experts to be literally stuffed with minerals. And if Perth has always been somewhat off the tourist map, that could be changing too: for it has dawned on airline passengers travelling from Europe (although not, I fear, on too many international airlines as yet) that Perth is only one stop and 18 hours away from home compared with the two stops and 25 hours needed to get from London to Sydney. Perth eventually may well become both one of Australia's most important commercial centres and one of its leading tourist destinations.

This is, perhaps, as it should be. For the coast of Western Australia was visited by some of the earliest European navigators ever to see Australia – and may even have been settled by a couple of Dutchmen, albeit involuntarily, when they were marooned on the mainland in 1629 as punishment for taking part in a mutiny. There are those who claim that this accounts for the European features of many of the local aboriginals in the area around Geraldton, 400 kilometres north of Perth.

Officially, Perth was founded on 12 August 1829, by Captain James Stirling and a group of settlers made up largely of ex-Army and ex-Naval officers. On a previous visit Stirling had realised the area's immense potential, but the British Government's decision to allow his settlement to go ahead was founded on more practical motives: there were serious fears that the French might attempt to colonise Western Australia as a counter-balance to the British colonies in the southeast.

Stirling's choice of site for his new settlement was faultless. He picked a spot 19 kilometres inland from the mouth of the Swan River, at a point where the river narrowed then widened again, so that there was virtually a freshwater lake on either side of the town. The present Town Hall stands very close to the spot where Stirling read out the proclamation founding the new town.

But things did not go well for the new colony. The aboriginals proved to be distinctly unfriendly, the crops failed, and in 1848 Western Australia was forced to ask Sydney for a supply of convict labour. Sydney responded by despatching a group of 9700 convicts to Perth – apparently oblivious of the fact that this would mean that convicts outnumbered free settlers by a ratio of two to one. The frightened citizens of Perth appealed to the British Government for help, and a further group of 5000 free settlers – including women – set sail from Britain for Perth to redress the balance.

But Western Australia remained the 'poor relation' of the continent for another half-century. Then, in the 1890s, gold was discovered in Kalgoorlie, 550 kilometres east of Perth – and, like

Western Australia

New South Wales and Victoria before it, the state experienced an immigration boom as newcomers rushed in to try to make their fortunes. And, in many ways, that boom has continued ever since – for further mineral discoveries, especially iron ore, nickel, uranium, bauxite, and natural gas, have ensured that the interest of the financial and industrial giants of the world in Western Australia is considerable. People and money have poured into the state. And the process could speed up even more if, as is expected, recoverable oil deposits are also found there.

All this has meant that Western Australia, despite its small population in relation to both its size and to the rest of Australia, is remarkably prosperous. Couple that prosperity with its somewhat tenuous links with the rest of the country (Adelaide is over four hours' flying time away, and the cross-country Indian Pacific train takes 65 hours to complete its four-times-a-week journey), and one can perhaps understand the enthusiasm on the part of some state politicians for Western Australia to declare itself independent of the rest of the country. In the long term, however, the federation is unlikely to break up, for Australia is a remarkably stable country and there is little real point in rocking the boat. One West Australian who disagrees is Leonard Casley, who has declared his farm north of Geraldton, 400 kilometres from Perth, to be an independent state called Hutt River. Mr Casley is the self-appointed 'Prince' of this 'state', which has a population of 30 and issues its own passports and postage stamps. The Hutt River Province was the subject of a fascinating television programme in Britain made by globetrotter Alan Whicker, whom Mr Casley appointed 'Ambassador to the Court of St James's' for his pains. The official state government seems unconcerned by such goings-on: no doubt it pulls in the tourists.

Perth, meanwhile, oozes opulence and peaceful contentment. A row of stately new skyscrapers lines St George's Terrace, overlooking the Swan River and the Narrows Bridge. But between and behind these office buildings and luxury hotels, a number of the city's more historic buildings remain, and perhaps serve as a reminder of less happy days. They include the Old Courthouse, in Stirling Gardens, built in 1836 in classic Georgian style and Perth's oldest building; the restored Old Gaol, in Francis Street, which dates from 1856 (open daily, and Sunday afternoons); The Cloisters, a brick-built boys' school built in St George's Terrace in 1858; part of the old Pensioners' Barracks, the former military headquarters in St

Western Australia

George's Terrace, which date from 1860; Governor Kennedy's Fountain, in Mount Bay Road (1861); the Romantic-style Government House, in St George's Terrace, which was completed in 1864; and the Town Hall on the corner of Hay Street and Barrack Street, dating from 1870. Many of these buildings were constructed wholly or partly by convict labour. Just across the Narrows Bridge another of Perth's first buildings, the Old Flour Mill, which was built in 1835 and has now been restored and contains a museum of antiques from the earliest days of Perth's settlement. It is open afternoons, except Tuesdays and Fridays.

Perth's principal building is, however, a more recent construction: the massive 8000-seat Entertainment Centre. This auditorium, the largest in Australia, combines with the smaller and more intimate Perth Concert Hall, and numerous theatres and theatre-restaurants, to present the cultural face of the city. Perth has good local opera, ballet and theatre companies, while the magnificent facilities at the Entertainment Centre coupled with enthusiastic audiences mean that Perth receives many visits from overseas performers. The arts are all very well supported, but it is only fair to add that visiting pop stars can (and do) also fill every one of the Entertainment Centre's seats. Also worth a place on every visitor's itinerary is the West Australian Art Gallery and Museum (open daily, and Sunday afternoons) which mysteriously mixes aboriginal and modern paintings with such exhibits as the skeleton of a Blue Whale and veteran and vintage cars.

But Perth is first and foremost an outdoor city, and this is emphasised not only by the meandering waterways of the Swan River, which dominate almost every view, but also by the fact that the city planners very wisely left undeveloped 400 hectares of virgin bushland right in the centre of the city: Kings Park. Kings Park is perhaps the most dramatic park to be found in any city in the world, for not only is it very close to the city centre, but its sheer size means that its character has not been changed by the encroachment of suburbia. It is heavily used, for it contains picnic and barbecue sites and children's playgrounds, besides providing some extremely photogenic views of the city centre and the river. But there are still walking trails through the bush, and glorious displays of wild flowers to supplement the more formal landscaped gardens. Houses overlooking the park and the river are among the most expensive in Australia – almost (but not quite) matching the price of some of Sydney's finest homes.

Western Australia

The river itself, beloved of yachtsmen (although it is not nearly as crowded with privately owned boats as Sydney Harbour), is very attractive as it winds its way down towards Fremantle. There are boat trips on the river, departing from the Ferry Terminal close to the town centre, but I think it is better seen from the shore. In fact the only thing missing from a view of the Swan River with the city skyline behind it is Western Australia's famous black swans. But you will not find them on the river which is their namesake: they prefer, instead, the faintly murky waters of Lake Monger, a hefty suburban pond just north of the city centre. If the setting disappoints, at least the swans will not: there are hundreds of them.

Hotel developments in the city are proceeding at such a pace that any advice might rapidly be out of date, but there are several top-grade hotels in Perth and there will eventually be many more. I like the Parmelia Hilton, in Mill Street, which is close to everything and has large, comfortable rooms. Restaurants vary immensely: the best are probably those at the Hilton and Sheraton hotels, but there are plenty of very good seafood restaurants, and a variety of ethnic restaurants in James Street, in the Northbridge area. Theatre-restaurants, mentioned earlier, are popular with the locals, but visitors may not enjoy them: I have yet to find one where both the play and the food were good, and you can hardly walk out of a bad play in the middle of your dinner – or vice versa. Besides Northbridge, there is a good choice of restaurants in Stirling Highway, the main street in Subiaco, and parts of Fremantle. Most restaurants are BYOGS (see Chapter 4). Nightlife generally is rather limited: there are bars, discos and nightclubs in the Northbridge area which, according to the tourist literature, will 'entertain you 'til the early hours'. In practice, the people of Perth seem to prefer early nights to a night on the tiles, and you are likely to find yourself back at your hotel rather sooner than you had intended.

En route down to Fremantle, by road or by river, one passes the Mediterranean-style buildings of the University of Western Australia, as well as the headquarters of the city's various yacht clubs. The mouth of the Swan River, Blackwall Reach, is crossed by bridge to reach Fremantle, Australia's principal Indian Ocean port. The port is, of course, crowded and busy, a venue for huge container ships. But, for a seaport, it is a remarkably clean, pleasant and friendly place – just the sort of port, in fact, which one would expect Perth to have. The back-street pubs are fascinating, and Western Australians more pleased to see you than their cousins in the southeast (although

Western Australia

they are also naturally rather reserved). The odd thing about Fremantle, I think, is standing beside the Indian Ocean and getting that edge-of-the-world feeling mentioned earlier.

But even if it were the edge of the world, there would at least be something out to sea. For there, on the horizon, 18 kilometres from Fremantle, is Rottnest Island, Western Australia's favourite and most unique holiday resort.

Rottnest Island is a completely informal island – 10 kilometres long, and anything from four kilometres to only a few metres wide – where cars are banned and everyone rides bicycles (you can hire one on the island, or bring one over on the ferry from the mainland). Somehow, it is an unexpected place to find in Australia. In an informal country, it stresses its own even greater informality – which means that nobody will bother you with rules and regulations. If you want to go into a meal barefoot, unshaven, and wearing only swimming trunks, then that is fine with Rottnest Island.

The island got its name from a Dutch explorer, Wilhelm Van Vlaming, who when he landed there in 1696 found it swarming with little grey furry creatures which he took to be rats. He called the island 'Rat's nest', and sailed away.

In fact, the little grey creatures are not rats at all, but quokkas – a very rare marsupial. And, because they are so friendly, they are one of the attractions of Rottnest.

Holidaymakers on the island can stay at 'the Quokka Arms', more formally known as the Rottnest Hotel, quite cheaply. There is sailing from the beach, overlooked by the hotel's beer garden, and a great variety of other sports are within easy reach by foot or by bicycle. There are secluded beaches everywhere for swimming and sunbathing, and the water round the island, protected by outer reefs, is always calm and clear. The most popular swimming beach is at The Basin, which is literally a basin in the rocky ocean bed. Fishing is excellent, be it from the beach, from a dinghy, with a spear, or a deep-sea chase after the famous black marlin. And there are daily trips out to the reef in a glass-bottomed boat.

Days on Rottnest Island speed by, but they also fit into a sort of pattern. Besides bicycles, Rottnest's other great institution is the bakery – outside which customers form daily queues for fresh bread, Rottnest Bakery doughnuts, pies, pasties and cream buns.

And then, at sunset, every visitor turns out to see the quokkas. They really are extraordinary little creatures: tame, friendly and cuddly. They emerge from their holes in search of food, and will eat

Western Australia

straight from your hand. But, just as you think you have won over your particular quokka, and will take him home as a pet, he will desert you for another hand holding another tasty titbit. Quokkas may be friendly, but they are very fickle too.

Besides Rottnest Island, excursions from Perth include the short trip up-river to the Swan Valley, the heart of Western Australia's wine-growing country (there are liberal tastings available, as elsewhere in the country), or down to the beaches. Perth's beaches of fine white sand really are extraordinary. The most popular ones are Cottesloe, Scarborough, City Beach and Trigg. Swanbourne is an unofficial nude beach. The surfing is often excellent along the coast, but swimming and sunbathing are popular too, and with such an endless succession of beaches it is always possible to find a stretch entirely to yourself.

Inland from Perth, running parallel to the coast, are the Darling Hills, another area popular with the townsfolk. Part of this region is national park-land, for the protection of flora and fauna, but there are plenty of pleasant walks and quiet picnic spots in the woods, and a handful of unexpected attractions. These include a reproduction of Shakespeare's birthplace in an 'Elizabethan' village serving Devonshire cream teas; Spanish Andalusian dancing stallions at El Caballo Blanco; open-air theatrical performances at the Parkerville Amphitheatre; and a number of 'pioneer' museums such as the one at Armadale. The Old Mahogany Inn, at Mahogany Creek, was built in 1842 as a military outpost to protect travellers between Perth and York from marauding aboriginals: it has now been restored and serves cream teas in the courtyard at weekends.

Beyond the Darling Range, the Avon Valley – of which York is the centre – is Western Australia's oldest inland settlement. The countryside is very like that of England, and the early settlers farmed it just as they would have done at home. Just outside York, Balladong Farm Living Musuem, the area's oldest farm, has been faithfully restored, and still works as it did 150 years ago: rearing the original breeds of sheep, pigs and cows, and using huge Clydesdale horses to pull the ploughs and power other farm machinery. Visitors can stay in the beautifully restored Old Settler's House, in York, where one dines by candlelight and a pianist in the Drawing Room provides what must surely be Australia's most gracious evening entertainment.

Like its namesake in England, the Avon is an attractive river, and the towns of the valley are attractive too. York has restored about a

Western Australia

dozen of its old buildings, including what is now the fascinating Residency Museum. Northiam is famous for its very un-Australian *white* swans, a gift from the village of the same name in England. And Beverley has a very good Aeronautical Museum, as well as a farming museum at the Avondale Research Station.

South of Perth are the city's other 'weekend resorts' – a string of beaches centred on the two main towns of Rockingham, about an hour's drive from Perth, and Mandurah, 30 minutes' farther on. Both towns have protected beaches which are safe for children, and the coastline is famous for its crabs (a favourite picnic lunch for local tourists is freshly cooked crabs bought at the roadside, fresh crusty bread, and cold beer). Mandurah is built around an estuary which widens into the beautiful Peel Inlet – an area of islets and reedy shores which can be explored by hired motorboat. Upstream the Ravenswood Hotel, one of the most picturesque hotels in Western Australia, is recommended.

To the north of Perth the seaside fishing and holiday towns are rather less sophisticated than those to the south: accommodation is at best in motels, but more probably in a rented holiday cottage or a caravan park, where you buy what you need from the local general store and cater for yourself. The area's charm seems to lie partly in its extremely relaxed atmosphere, partly in its fishing opportunities, and partly in the fact that most beaches are protected by a reef and are therefore safe for children.

But the tourist cars and coaches do head north because in the Nambung National Park, near the fishing harbour of Cervantes, can be seen one of the most unique landscapes in the world: the eerie rock formations of the Pinnacles. Here, in a wasteland of white sand drifts, oddly shaped limestone barbs rise abruptly out of the ground. Some of these 'pinnacles' are up to 12 metres high, and the rock surfaces have been etched away by the wind to reveal coverings of fossilised twigs. Both the rocks and the sand change colour at the beginning and end of the day, and the whole landscape has a strange, unearthly feel about it. The track from Cervantes to the Pinnacles is sometimes closed by heavy rain, so check in the village before setting out.

The sheer size of Western Australia suggests the average tourist is most unlikely to venture farther north than the Pinnacles. Geraldton, another 200 kilometres to the north, is a pleasant resort which Western Australians sometimes flee to in search of a winter suntan, and it has excellent hotel accommodation and restaurants – not to

Western Australia

mention a lively Sunshine Festival every September. The village of Greenough, just south of Geraldton, is preserved by the National Trust as a typical Western Australian early farming community. But beyond Geraldton one is into stretches of fishing coast backed by sheep farming country (some sheep stations are willing to accommodate tourists and let them join in the station's work). Farther north still are the massive iron and mineral deposits of the Pilbara: and it is here that those massive 220-tonne trucks, with wheels 2.7 metres across, which are sometimes seen in television advertisements, actually exist and work. Port Hedland is the principal port of the Pilbara, and does have modern accommodation.

In the far north of the state lie the West Kimberley and East Kimberley regions – the former being one of the oldest geological areas on earth, with rocks estimated at 2500 million years old. Time and weather have worn deep gorges into the hills, and the coastal sandstone on the coast is rich in fossils (naturalists have even found the footprint of a dinosaur, left in the rock some 130 million years ago). The port of Broome was once a pearling centre, and as such attracted pearl divers from all over the Far East. Today pearl fishing is a tiny industry, the scientists having discovered ways of making pearls rather more perfect than those which the oyster can produce. But Broome's Oriental atmosphere lingers on in its interesting old Chinatown district. Just outside the region's other port, Derby, is a remarkable oddity: a hollowed out baobab tree which used to serve as a temporary gaol. Geikie Gorge, near Fitzroy Crossing, 250 kilometres inland from Derby, is the region's leading beauty spot – and would probably be a tourist trap if it were anywhere else in the world. As it is, visitors will have to work hard to reach the gorge – where a cruise boat, or a walking track, follow the course of the river through a densely wooded gorge rich in wildlife. East Kimberley has had its rugged character changed somewhat in the past 20 years, with the development of an irrigation scheme in the Ord River Valley. Besides producing rich farmland, this scheme produced a very pleasant, if somewhat inaccessible, tropical holiday resort too. The main town is Kununurra, a very appropriate aboriginal word meaning 'big waters', and there is a self-contained holiday village overlooking the huge Lake Argyle, 50 kilometres by road from Kununurra. The winter weather is glorious, but one might find the local crocodiles something of a deterrent. And finally, if one did happen to be touring this area, it might just be worth taking the 800-kilometres round trip detour to Wolf Creek Crater – an immense

Western Australia

hole left in the desert by a giant meteorite which collided with the Earth 50,000 years ago. One thing: the meteorite could hardly have chosen a more remote spot.

To the southeast and east of Perth there is slightly more to see in the way of scenery; slightly less to see as far as the noteworthy is concerned. Albany, on the southern tip of Western Australia, is an extremely pretty port overlooking the deep-water port of Princess Royal Harbour. The accommodation, beaches, and fishing are good, and the view of the town from Mount Melville Lookout is a memorable one. There is plenty of attractive countryside in this region, too – green and pastoral. Farther east, anyone making the road journey to Adelaide should make a detour to Esperance with its magnificent cliff scenery in and around Cape le Grand National Park.

The most extraordinary sight in the southern part of Western Australia – and perhaps in the state as a whole – is the Wave Rock, near Hayden. Shaped like a huge wave about to break over the countryside, the granite rock is several hundred metres long and an estimated 2700 million years old. It looks like becoming Western Australia's biggest tourist attraction outside Perth, and tourist facilities – including a caravan park, a wildlife sanctuary and a golf course – are springing up around it.

But it has a rival of a very different kind in the shape of the twin mining towns of Kalgoorlie and Boulder, in the centre of the southern half of the state.

Between Kalgoorlie and Boulder lies what is almost certainly the richest square mile of ground in the world: the Golden Mile. There, on 15 June 1893, an Irish prospector called Paddy Hannan found a series of sandy gullies in which gold nuggets could just be picked off the surface. He and two colleagues collected 200 ounces of gold in only a few days, and as word of their good fortune spread an enormous gold rush began. Many prospectors shared Paddy Hannan's fortune, for the goldfield was eventually to yield more than 40 million ounces of the precious metal.

You can still see Paddy Hannan, for his bronze statue stands outside the town hall – dispensing drinking water from his water bag, which doubles as a fountain. The main street bears his name, and so does a local beer. He certainly brought fame and prosperity to a town which, at the height of its fame, boasted 92 hotels. But as some of the outer goldfields dried up, mines were closed and satellite towns deserted. Kalgoorlie and Boulder could have slipped quietly into history.

Western Australia

In a way, they have. The twin towns are partly a living museum, complete with restored historic buildings and an authentic mine. Get a miner's right from the Mines Department and you can even go prospecting for yourself – with pick and shovel, a traditional gold pan, or even a modern metal detector if you wish.

Kalgoorlie will be pleased if you do find anything, and not a whit jealous. For just as the city seemed doomed to become another ghost town, like so many of its neighbours, there was a nickel boom, and Kalgoorlie has nickel a-plenty. What is more, rising gold prices have also started to make gold-mining a worthwhile venture there, too.

It could be very worthwhile indeed. Local rumour has it that less than half of Kalgoorlie's gold has so far been extracted from the ground. And if that is true, another Paddy Hannan may strike it rich one day soon. The visitor with his metal detector could be on to a very good thing indeed.

An exciting present, and the prospect of a glittering future. That seems an apt way in which to sum up Western Australia.

It might also be a convenient way in which to sum up the nation as a whole. Big, lovely Australia is a country with everything, and it knows that it has a great future. But it also knows that the future has to be worked for – which is why work-shy 'bludgers' and 'sundowners' get short shrift from Australians. The Australians work hard and play hard, which perhaps is why – at least until now – they have had little time for 'entertaining' you, the visitor from overseas.

Now they would like you to come and see them, but....

That 'but' had been bothering me. The Australians have always been, and still are, slightly diffident in their dealings with anyone from overseas. They have seemed to be trying to say something, yet did not quite know how to put it.

After thousands of miles of travel, all around Australia, I think I know what that is. They are saying, as a nation, to overseas visitors, tourist and holidaymakers: 'Come on over, mate; but you'll have to take us as you find us.'

Index

Cape York Peninsula, 142, 143
Carnarvon Ranges, 133
Carpentaria, Gulf of, 143
Casely, Leonard, 159
Castlereagh, 77
Chain of Lagoons, 125
Charleville, 152
Christies Beach, 103
Cockington Green, 63
Conara Junction, 125
constitution, 17–19
Coober, Pedy, 108
Cook, Capt. James, 28, 87, 98, 113, 134, 135, 142
Cooktown, 138, 142
Coolangatta, 127
Coomera, 126, 127
Coonabarabran, 81
Cooper Creek, 134
Copping, 117
cricket, 14, 47, 84, 85
Cumberland Islands, 135–138
currency, 22
Currumbin Sanctuary, 130
Cygnet, 121

Dandenong Ranges, 92
Dare, John, 146, 156
Darling Hills, 163
Darwin, 30, 97, 146–147, 154
Daydream Island, 138
Derby, 165
Derwent Bridge, 124
Derwent River, 113, 115, 116, 123
Devonport, 111, 123
Dieman, Anthony van, 112
dingo, 36
diprotodon, 25, 108
Doo Town, 118
Dover, 121
Dreamtime, the, 26–27, 145, 146
Dreamworld, 126–127
Dunalley, 118
Dunk Island, 138

Eaglehawk Neck, 118
Elephany Pass, 125
emus, 37, 38
Esperance, 166
Eyre, Edward, 29

Fitzroy Crossing, 165
Fleming, Thomas, 142

Flinders, Matthew, 29, 104
Flinders Island, 114
Flinders Ranges, 24, 97, 101, 105
Flinders Street station, 83, 84, 91
Flying Doctor Service, Royal, 82, 143, 150–152
Flynn, Errol, 115
Fraser Island, 133
Fremantle, 160–162
French Island, 91
Friendly Beaches, the, 124, 125

Geelong, 92
Geike Gorge, 165
Geraldton, 159, 164
Ginninnderra Falls, 63
Gippsland worm, 39
Gladstone, 139
Gold Coast, 47, 128, 130
Golsen, Professor Jack, 25
Goolwa, 105
Gosford, 76
Grafton, 79-80
Gramp, Johann, 105
Great Barrier Reef, 9, 22, 41, 132, 134–139
Great Dividing Range, 52, 93
Great Keppel Island, 138
Green Island, 138
Greenough, 164
Greenway, Francis, 68
Griffin, Walter Burley, 53, 55, 66
Grose, Major Francis, 29, 68
Gudgenby Nature Reserve, 64

Hamilton, John, 35, 118
Hannan, Paddy, 167
Hartz Mountains, 121
Hayman Island, 135, 137–138
Healesville, 92, 93
Heron Island, 135
Hinchingbrook Island, 138
Hindmarsh, Capt. John, 98, 100
Hobart, 111–114, 121, 123, 124
    buildings, 116
    docks, 115
    gambling, 115–116
    museums, 116–117
Hook Island, 137
horse-racing, 47
Hunter Valley, 79
Hutt River Province, 159

Index

ichtyostega, 24, 25
immigration, 30, 31

Kadumalu, 145, 146
Kalgoorlie, 152, 158, 166–167
Kangaroo Island, 37, 97–98, 104
kangaroos, 36–37
Katherine Gorge, 148
Katoomba, 78
Kelly, Ned, 30, 87
Kempton, 121, 122
Kimberley, East, 165
Kimberley, West, 165
koalas, 38, 132
Kondalilla National Park, 133
kookaburras, 39, 41
Korralbyn, 130
Kunumurra, 165
Kuranda, 141
Kwinana, 157

Lady Elliott Island, 134
Lake Callabonna, 108
Lake Eyre, 108
Lamington National Park, 130
Launceston, 111, 112, 114, 121–125
   accommodation, 123
   buildings, 123
Light, Col. William, 98, 99, 100
Lightning Ridge, 82
Lindeman Island, 138
Lizard Island, 138
Lone Pine Koala Sanctuary, 38, 132
Long Island, 138
Longhurst, John, 126, 127
Longreach, 133
lyre birds, 41

McCullough, Colleen, 135
Mackay, 135, 140
Macquarie, Lachlan, 29, 77
Macquarie, Lake, 79
Maetracci, André, 137
Magnetic Island, 138
Mahogany Creek, 163
Mandeville, Sir John, 26, 28
Mandurah, 164
Mannum, 105
Marree, 109
Maslin Beach, 101, 103
Melbourne, 9, 16, 22, 52, 83–91
   buildings, 88–90
   Cricket Ground, 84

hotels, 90
Melbourne Age, the 85
museums, 87
parks, 86, 87
restaurants, 90–91
shopping, 90
Menglers Hill, 105
Menzies, Sir Robert, 60
Merimbula, 81
Mermaid Beach, 128
Miami, 128
Mildura, 96
Millaa Millaa Falls, 141
Millstream Falls, 141
Monger, Lake, 160
Montgomery, Lord, 115
Moreton Bay, 131, 132
Moreton Island, 132
Morgan, 105
Mossman, 142
Mount Coot-tha, 131, 132
Mount Donna Buang, 93
Mount Gamber, 104, 105
Mount Isa, 143, 152
Mount Lofty Ranges, 98, 100, 103
Mountford, Charles, 26
Murray Bridge, 105
Murray River, 23, 81, 96, 97, 98, 107, 108
Murrumbidgee River, 64, 81, 98

Nambour, 134
Nerang River, 128, 130
New Norfolk, 123, 124
Newcastle, 79
Noosa Heads, 132
Nullarbor Plain, 29, 157
Numinbah Valley, 130
Nuriootpa, 105

Oatlands, 121, 122
Oberon, Merle, 115
Olga Mountains, 24, 145, 152, 155
Ord River Valley, 165
Ormiston Gorge, 152, 155, 156
Orpheus Island, 138

Palm Valley, 155
Paterson, 'Banjo', 134
Peel Inlet, 164
Perth, 16, 22, 108, 157–160
   buildings, 159
   entertainments, 160

171

Index

Perth—*cont.*
  hotels, 160
  Kings Park, 160
  museums, 160
  nightlife, 160
  restaurants, 160
  Town Hall, 158, 159
Phillip, Capt. Arthur, 28, 29, 77
Phillip Island, 41, 91
Picton, 78
Pilbara, the, 165
Pineapple, the Big, 134
Pinnacles, the, 164
Pitt Town, 77
platypus, 25, 39
Port Augusta, 106
Port Arthur, 112, 113, 114, 117–120
Port Campbell, 92
Port Douglas, 142
Port Hedland, 165
Port Lincoln, 98
Port Macquarie, 79
Port Noarlunga, 103
Port Phillip Bay, 83, 91, 92
Port Stephens, 79
Proserpine, 134, 140

Qantas, 21, 22, 23, 35, 134
Queenstown, 123, 124

railways, 22, 81, 84, 108, 140, 143, 154
Ravenshoe, 141
Renmark, 105
Richmond (NSW), 77
Richmond (Tasmania), 117
Robinson, George, 114
Rockhampton, 135, 138, 139, 140
Rockingham, 164
Roma, 133
Ross, 121, 122
Rottnest Island, 162–163

School of the Air, 82, 152
Seppelt, Joseph, 105
Shute Harbour, 135
Shute, Nevil, 148
Simpson's Gap, 154
Smith, Jack, 117
South Molle Island, 138
Sovereign Hill, 95, 96
Springbrook Plateau, 130
Stanley, 124
Stanley Chasm, 154

Stirling, Capt. James, 158
Strathgordon, 124
Sturt, Capt. Charles, 29, 98
Sunshine Coast, 132
Surfers Paradise, 23, 126–130
  entertainments, 129, 130
  hotels, 129
Swan Reach, 105
Swan River, 157, 158, 159, 160, 161
Swan Valley, 163
Sydney, 9, 13, 16, 22, 30, 52, 67–75
  beaches, 67, 74
  buildings, 68, 71, 72, 75
  Harbour, 68, 69
  Harbour Bridge, 67, 69, 71
  hotels, 73
  Kings Cross, 67, 72
  museums, 72, 73
  nightlife, 71, 72, 74
  Opera House, 13, 67, 69, 70, 71
  restaurants, 71, 74
  Rocks, the, 67, 69, 71
  shopping, 71, 73

Tambourine Mountain, 130
Tamworth, 80
Tanunda, 105
Tasman, Abel, 28, 112, 113, 118
Tasman Bridge, 116
Tasman Peninsula, 117–120
Tasmanian devil, 34, 36, 118
Tasmanian tiger, 34, 35
Thorne, Dr Alan, 25
Thredbo, 65
Thursday Island, 142
Tidbinbilla, 64
tipping, 49
Toowoomba, 133
Torres, Luis Vaez de, 142
Torres Strait, 142
Torres Strait Islands, 142
Townsville, 138, 140
Tweed Heads, 79, 127
Tweed Valley, 80
Tunbridge, 121, 122

Ulverston, 123

Vaucluse House, 75, 76
Victor Harbour, 103

Wagga Wagga, 81
Wakefield, Edward Gibbon, 98

Index

Wallaman Falls, 141
Waltzing Matilda, 134
Warrnambool, 92
Wellington, Mount, 117
Welpa, 142
Wentworth, William, 29, 76
Westernport Bay, 91
Whicker, Alan, 159
Whitsunday Islands, 135–138
Wilberforce, 77
Willunga, 103

Wilpena Pound, 105
Windsor, 77
Winton, 134
Wilson's Promontory, 91
Wolf Creek Crater, 165
Wollongong, 80
Woomera, 108

Yarra River, 85, 88
Yarrawonga Park, 147
York, 163, 164